Geometry Connections Parent Guide

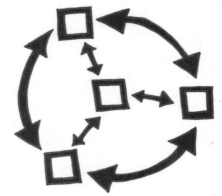

Managing Editor

Leslie Dietiker
Phillip and Sala Burton Academic High School
San Francisco, CA

Contributing Editors

Elizabeth Ellen Coyner
Christian Brothers High School
Sacramento, CA

Lew Douglas
The College Preparatory School
Oakland, CA

David Gulick
Phillips Exeter Academy
Exeter, NH

Lara Lomac
Phillip and Sala Burton Academic
High School, San Francisco, CA

Damian Molinari
Phillip and Sala Burton Academic
High School, San Francisco, CA

Jason Murphy-Thomas
George Washington High School
San Francisco, CA

Leslie Nielsen
Isaaquah High School
Issaquah, WA

Karen O'Connell
San Lorenzo High School
San Lorenzo, CA

Ward Quincey
Gideon Hausner Jewish Day School
Palo Alto, CA

Barbara Shreve
San Lorenzo High School
San Lorenzo, CA

Michael Titelbaum
University of California
Berkeley, CA

Illustrator

Kevin Coffey
San Francisco, CA

Technical Assistants

Erica Andrews

Elizabeth Burke

Carrie Cai

Daniel Cohen

Elizabeth Fong

Rebecca Harlow

Michael Leong

Thomas Leong

Marcos Rojas

Susan Ryan

Program Directors

Leslie Dietiker
Phillip and Sala Burton Academic High School
San Francisco, CA

Judy Kysh, Ph.D.
Departments of Mathematics and Education
San Francisco State University

Brian Hoey
Christian Brothers High School
Sacramento, CA

Tom Sallee, Ph.D.
Department of Mathematics
University of California, Davis

Editors of the Parent Guide:

Karen Wootten, Managing Editor
Odenton, MD

Brian Hoey
Sacramento, CA

Technical Manager of Parent Guide and Extra Practice:

Rebecca Harlow
Stanford University
Stanford, CA

Editor of Extra Practice:

Bob Petersen, Managing Editor
Rosemont High School
Sacramento, CA

Assessment Contributors:

John Cooper, Managing Editor
Del Oro High School
Loomis, CA

Damian Molinari
Phillip and Sala Burton Academic High School
San Francisco, CA

Leslie Dietiker
Phillip and Sala Burton Academic High School
San Francisco, CA

Barbara Shreve
San Lorenzo High School
San Lorenzo, CA

2 3 4 5 6 7 8 9   10 09

Printed in the United States of America

ISBN-10:   1-931287-62-7

ISBN-13: 978-1-931287-62-3

Introduction to the Parent Guide

Welcome to the *Algebra Connections Parent Guide*. The purpose of this guide is to assist you should your child need help with homework or the ideas in the course. We believe all students can be successful in mathematics as long as they are willing to work and ask for help when they need it. We encourage you to contact your child's teacher if your student has additional questions that this guide or other resources do not answer. **Assistance with most homework problems is available at www.hotmath.com.**

This guide was written to address the major topics in each chapter of the textbook. Each section of the Parent Guide begins with a title bar and the section(s) of the book that it addresses. In many cases the explanation box at the beginning of the section refers you to one or more Math Notes boxes in the student text for additional information about the fundamentals of the idea. Detailed examples follow a summary of the concept or skill and include complete solutions. The examples are similar to the work your child has done in class. Additional problems, with answers, are provided for your child to practice. Additional problems are available in the *Geometry Connections Extra Practice Booklet*. It is available for download or purchase at www.cpm.org

There will be some topics that your child understands quickly and some concepts that may take longer to master. The big ideas of the course take time to learn. This means that students are not necessarily expected to master a concept when it is first introduced. When a topic is first introduced in the textbook, there will be several problems to do for practice. Subsequent lessons and homework assignments will continue to practice the concept or skill over weeks and months so that <u>mastery</u> <u>will</u> <u>develop</u> <u>over</u> <u>time</u>.

Practice and discussion are required to understand mathematics. When your child comes to you with a question about a homework problem, often you may simply need to ask your child to read the problem and then ask her/him what the problem is asking. Reading the problem aloud is often more effective than reading it silently. When you are working problems together, have your child talk about the problems. Then have your child practice on his/her own.

Below is a list of additional questions to use when working with your child. These questions do not refer to any particular concept or topic. Some questions may or may not be appropriate for some problems.

- What have you tried? What steps did you take?
- What didn't work? Why didn't it work?
- What have you been doing in class or during this chapter that might be related to this problem?
- What does this word/phrase tell you?
- What do you know about this part of the problem?
- Explain what you know right now.
- What do you need to know to solve the problem?
- How did the members of your study team explain this problem in class?
- What important examples or ideas were highlighted by your teacher?
- Can you draw a diagram or sketch to help you?
- Which words are most important? Why?
- What is your guess/estimate/prediction?
- Is there a simpler, similar problem we can do first?

- How did you organize your information? Do you have a record of your work?
- Have you tried Guess and Check, making a list, looking for a pattern, etc.?

If your student has made a start at the problem, try these questions.

- What do you think comes next? Why?
- What is still left to be done?
- Is that the only possible answer?
- Is that answer reasonable?
- How could you check your work and your answer?
- How could your method work for other problems?

If you do not seem to be making any progress, you might try these questions.

- Let's look at your notebook, class notes, and Learning Log. Do you have them?
- Were you listening to your team members and teacher in class? What did they say?
- Did you use the class time working on the assignment? Show me what you did.
- Were the other members of your team having difficulty with this as well? Can you call your study partner or someone from your study team?

This is certainly not a complete list; you will probably come up with some of your own questions as you work through the problems with your child. Ask any question at all, even if it seems too simple to you.

To be successful in mathematics, students need to develop the ability to reason mathematically. To do so, students need to think about what they already know and then connect this knowledge to the new ideas they are learning. Many students are not used to the idea that what they learned yesterday or last week will be connected to today's lesson. Too often students do not have to do much thinking in school because they are usually just told what to do. When students understand that connecting prior learning to new ideas is a normal part of their education, they will be more successful in this mathematics course (and any other course, for that matter). The student's responsibilities for learning mathematics include the following:

- Actively contributing in whole class and study team work and discussions.
- Completing (or at least attempting) all assigned problems and turning in assignments in a timely manner.
- Checking and correcting problems on assignments (usually with their study partner or study team) based on answers and solutions provided in class.
- Studying the tutorial solutions to homework problems available at www.hotmath.com.
- Asking for help when needed from his or her study partner, study team, and/or teacher.
- Attempting to provide help when asked by other students.
- Taking notes and using his/her Learning Log when recommended by the teacher or the text.
- Keeping a well-organized notebook.
- Not distracting other students from the opportunity to learn.

Assisting your child to understand and accept these responsibilities will help him or her to be successful in this course, develop mathematical reasoning, and form habits that will help her/him become a life-long learner.

Table of Contents

By asking questions such as "What happens if…?" and "What if I change this…?" and answering them by trying different things, we can find out quite a lot of information about different shapes. In the first five sections of this first chapter, we explore symmetry, making predictions, perimeter, area, logical arguments, and angles by investigating each of them with interesting problems. These five sections are introductory and help the teacher determine students' prior knowledge and preview some of the ideas that will be studied in this course. The following examples illustrate the geometry ideas in this section as well as some of the algebra review topics.

See the Math Notes Boxes on pages 5, 10, 15, 19, and 24.

Example 1

Suppose the rug in Figure 1 is enlarged as shown.

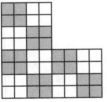

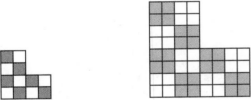

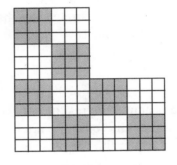

one unit

one square unit

Figure 1   Figure 2   Figure 3

Fill in the table below to show how the perimeter and the area of the rug change as it is enlarged.

Figure Number	1	2	3	4	5	20
Perimeter (in units)						
Area (in square units)						

The perimeter of a figure is the distance (length) around the outside of the figure while the area measures the surface within the figure. The area is measured in square units while the perimeter is simply a unit of length, such as inches or centimeters. Counting the units around the outside of Figure 1, we get a perimeter of 16 units. By counting the number of square units within Figure 1, we find the area is 12 square units. We do the same for the next two figures and record the information in the table, then look for a pattern in the data.

Figure Number	1	2	3	4	5	20
Perimeter (in units)	16	32	48			
Area (in square units)	12	48	108			

Now comes the task of finding a pattern from these numbers. The perimeters seem to be connected to the number 16, while the areas seem connected to 12. Using this observation, we can rewrite the table and then extend the pattern to complete it as shown in the table below.

Figure Number	1	2	3	4	5	20
Perimeter (in units)	1(16)	2(16)	3(16)	4(16)	5(16)	20(16)
Area (in square units)	1(12)	4(12)	9(12)	16(12)	25(12)	400(12)

Notice that the first multiplier for the area is the square of the figure number.

Example 2

By using a hinged mirror and a piece of paper, the students explored how a kaleidoscope works. Through this investigation, the students saw how angles are related to shapes. In particular, by placing the hinge of the mirror at a certain angle, the students could create shapes with a specific number of sides. The hinge represents the angle at the center (or central angle) of the shape. (See pages 21 and 22 in the student text.) How many sides would the resulting shape have if the mirror is placed (1) as an acute angle (less than 90°)? (2) as a right angle (exactly 90°)? (3) as an obtuse angle (between 90° and 180°)?

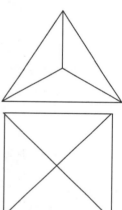

If the central angle is acute, the resulting figure is a triangle, so figures formed with this kind of angle are limited to three sides. As the hinge opens further and forms a right angle, the figure adds another side, creating a quadrilateral. If the two edges of the mirror have the same length on the paper, the quadrilateral is a square.

As the hinge opens even further, the angle it makes is now obtuse. This will create more and more sides on the shape as the angle increases in size. It is possible to create a pentagon (five sided figure), a hexagon (six sided figure), and, in fact, any number of sides using obtuse angles of increasing measures. If the hinge is straight across, it forms a straight angle (measuring 180°), and the figure is no longer a closed shape, but a line.

Example 3

Solve the equation for x: $2(x-4)+3(x+1)=43+x$

$$2(x-4)+3(x+1)=43+x \quad \text{Distribute}$$
$$2x-8+3x+3=43+x$$

In solving equations such as the one above, we simplify, combine like terms, and collect the variables on one side of the equal sign and the numbers on the other side.

$$5x-5=43+x \quad \text{Simplify}$$
$$4x=48 \quad \text{Divide by 4}$$
$$\frac{4x}{4}=\frac{48}{4}$$
$$x=12$$

The Methods and Meanings Math Notes box on page 19 also explains this process.

Problems

Find the perimeter and area of each shape below.

1.

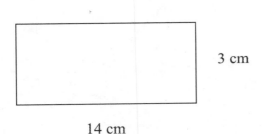

3 cm

14 cm

2.

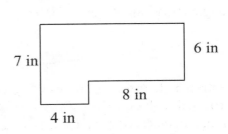

7 in   6 in

8 in

4 in

3.

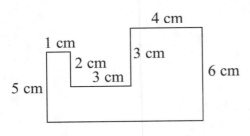

4 cm

1 cm   3 cm

2 cm

3 cm

5 cm   6 cm

4.

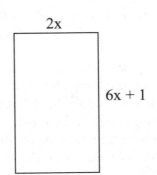

2x

6x + 1

5. If the perimeter for the rectangle for problem 4 is 34 units, write an equation and solve for x.

6. Solve for x. Show the steps leading to your solution. $-2x+6=5x-8$

7. Solve for x. Show the steps leading to your solution. $3(2x-1)+9=4(x+3)$

For problems 8-11, estimate the size of each angle to the nearest 10°. A right angle is shown for reference so you should not need a protractor. Then classify each angle as either acute, right, obtuse, straight, or circular.

8.

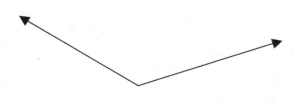

9.

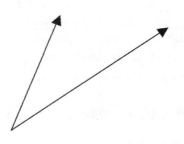

10.

11.

Answers

1. Perimeter = 34 cm, Area = 42 square cm

2. Perimeter = 38 in., Area = 76 sq in.

3. Perimeter = 32 cm, Area = 38 square cm

4. Perimeter = $16x + 2$ un, Area = $2x(6x + 1)$ or $12x^2 + 2x$ un^2

5. $2(2x) + 2(6x + 1) = 34$, $x = 2$

6. $x = 2$

7. $x = 3$

8. $\approx 160°$, obtuse

9. $\approx 40°$, acute

10. $180°$, straight

11. $90°$, right

Studying transformations of geometric shapes builds a foundation for a key idea in geometry: congruence. In this introduction to transformations, the students explore three rigid motions: translation, reflection, and rotation. This exploration is done with simple tools that can be found at home (tracing paper) as well as with computer software. Students create a new shape by applying one or more of these motions to the original figure to create its image in a new position without changing its size or shape. Transformations also lead directly to studying symmetry in shapes. These ideas will help with describing and classifying geometric shapes later in the chapter.

See the Math Notes boxes on pages 5, 34, 38, and 42.

Example 1

Decide which transformation was used on each pair of shapes below. Some may be a combination of transformations.

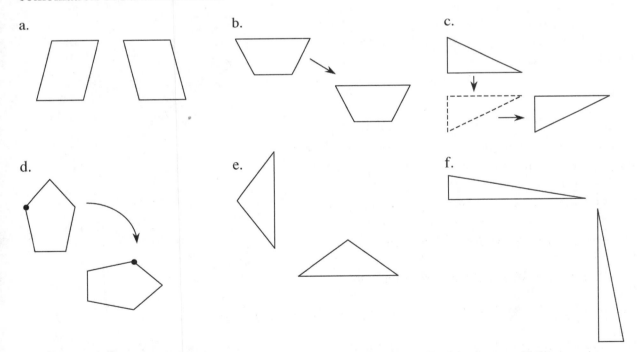

a.

b.

c.

d.

e.

f.

Identifying a single transformation is usually easy for students. In (a), the parallelogram is reflected (flipped) across an invisible vertical line. (Imagine a mirror running vertically between the two figures. One figure would be the reflection of the other.) Reflecting a shape once changes its orientation, that is, how its parts "sit" on the flat surface. For example, in (a), the two sides of the figure at left slant upwards to the right, whereas in its reflection at right, they slant upwards to the left. Likewise, the angles in the figure at left "switch positions" in the figure at right. In (b), the shape is translated (or slid) to the right and down. The orientation is the same.

Part (c) shows a combination of transformations. First the triangle is reflected (flipped) across an invisible horizontal line. Then it is translated (slid) to the right. The pentagon in part (d) has been rotated (turned) clockwise to create the second figure. Imagine tracing the first figure on tracing paper, then holding the tracing paper with a pin at one point below the first pentagon, then turning the paper to the right 90°. The second pentagon would be the result. Some students might see this as a reflection across a diagonal line. The pentagon itself could be, but with the added dot (small circle), the entire shape cannot be a reflection. If it had been reflected, the dot would have to be on the corner below the one shown in the rotated figure. The triangles in part (e) are rotations of each other (90° again). Part (f) shows another combination. The triangle is rotated (the horizontal side becomes vertical) but also reflected since the hypotenuse of the triangle (the longest side) points in the opposite direction from the first figure.

Example 2

What will the figure at right look like if it is first reflected across line *l* and then the result is reflected across line *m*?

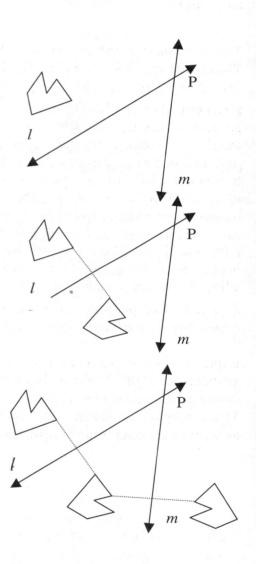

Just as the name implies, a reflection is the image of the shape. First we want to imagine that line *l* is a mirror. What would the image of the shape look like through this mirror?

The reflection is the new figure shown between the two lines. If we were to join each vertex (corner) of the original figure to its corresponding vertex on the second figure, those line segments would be perpendicular to line *l* and the vertices of (and all the other points in) the reflection would be the same distance away from *l* as they are in the original figure. One way to draw the reflection is to use tracing paper to trace the figure and the line *l*. Then turn the tracing paper over, so that line *l* is on top of itself. This will show the position of the reflection. Transfer the figure to your paper by tracing it. Repeat this process with line *m* to trace the third figure.

As we discovered in class, reflecting twice like this across two intersecting lines produces a **rotation** of the figure about the point P. Put the tracing paper back over the original figure to line *l*. Put a pin or the point of a pen or pencil on the tracing paper at point *P* and rotate the tracing paper until the original figure will fit perfectly on top of the last figure.

Example 3

The shape at right is trapezoid ABCD. Find the coordinates of each vertex of this trapezoid. Translate the trapezoid seven units to the right and four units up. Label the new trapezoid A'B'C'D' and give the coordinates of the four vertices. Is it possible to translate the original trapezoid in such a way to create A″B″C″D″ so that it is a reflection of ABCD? If so, what would be the reflecting line? Will this always be possible?

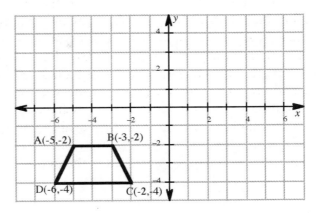

The coordinates of the trapezoid are A(-5, -2), B(-3, -2), C(-2, -4), and D(-6, -4). Translating (or sliding) the trapezoid seven units to the right and four units up gives a new trapezoid A'(2, 2), B'(4, 2), C'(5, 0) and D'(1, 0). If we forget about trapezoid A'B'C'D' for a moment and go back to ABCD, we now wonder if we can translate it in such a way that we can make it look as if it were a reflection rather than a translation. Since the trapezoid is symmetrical, it is possible to do so. We can slide the trapezoid horizontally left or right. In either case, the resulting figure would look like a reflection. This will not always work. It works here because the trapezoid we started with has a line of symmetry itself. The students

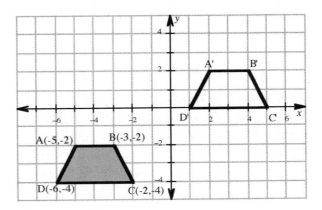

explored which polygons have lines of symmetry, and which have rotational symmetry as well. Again they used tracing paper as well as computer software to investigate these properties.

Exploring these transformations and symmetrical properties of shapes helps to improve students' visualization skills. These skills are often neglected or taken for granted, but much of mathematics requires the students to visualize a picture, problem, or situation in order to solve it. That is why we ask students to "visualize" or "imagine" what something might look like as well as practice creating some transformations of figures.

Problems

Perform the indicated transformation on each polygon below to create a new figure. You may want to use tracing paper to see how the figure moves.

1. Rotate figure A 90° clockwise about the origin.

2. Reflect figure B across line *l*.

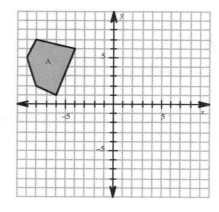

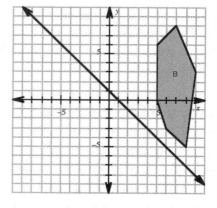

3. Translate figure C six units to the left.

4. Rotate figure D 270° clockwise about the origin (0, 0).

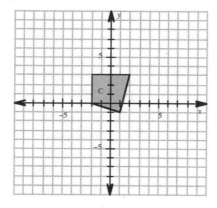

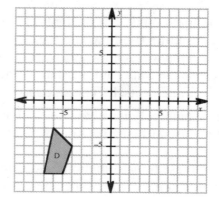

5. Plot the points A(3, 3), B(6, 1), and C(3, -4). Translate the triangle eight units to the left and one unit up to create ΔA'B'C'. What are the coordinates of this new triangle?

6. How can you translate ΔABC in the last problem to put point *A"* at (4, -5)?

7. Reflect Z across line *l*, and then reflect the new figure across line *m*. What are these two reflections equivalent to?

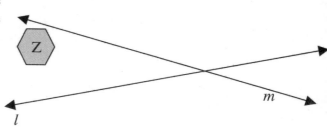

For each shape below, (*i*) draw all lines of symmetry, and (*ii*) describe its rotational symmetry if it exists.

8.

9.

10.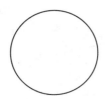

11.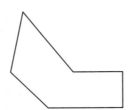

Answers

1. Rotate figure A 90° clockwise about the origin.

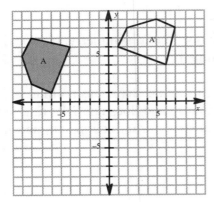

2. Reflect figure B across line *l*.

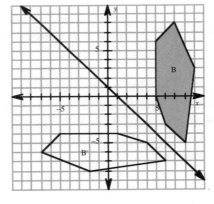

3. Translate figure C six units to the left.

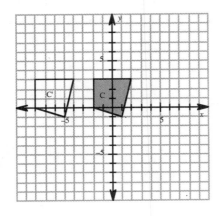

4. Rotate figure D 270° clockwise about the origin (0, 0).

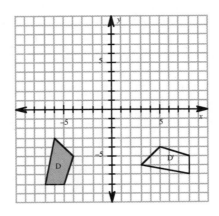

5.   A'(5, -4), B'(-2, 2), C'(-5, -3)

6.   Translate it one unit to the right and eight units down.

7.   The two reflections are the same as rotating Z about point X.

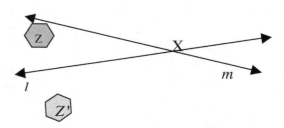

8.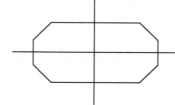

This has 180° rotational symmetry.

9.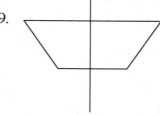

The one line of symmetry. No rotational symmetry.

10.   The circle has infinitely many lines of symmetry, everyone of them illustrates reflection symmetry. It also has rotational symmetry for every possible degree measure.

11.   This irregular shape has no lines of symmetry and does not have rotational symmetry, nor reflection symmetry.

Geometric shapes occur in many places. After studying them using transformations, students are starting to see certain characteristics of different shapes. In these sections we look at shapes more closely, noticing similarities and differences. We begin to classify them using Venn Diagrams. Students begin to see the need for accurate names, which expands our geometric vocabulary. The last section introduces probability.

See the Math Notes boxes on pages 51 and 60.

Example 1

Using all the shapes listed on resource page 1.2.5, show which shapes belong in each section on the Venn diagram below.

#1: Has only two pairs of parallel sides

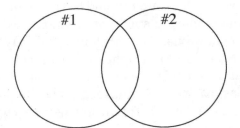

#2: Has all sides the same length

The left circle, circle #1, represents all those shapes on the resource page that have only two pairs of parallel sides. There are four figures on the resource page that have this characteristic: the rectangle, the square, the rhombus, and the parallelogram. These shapes will be contained in circle #1. Circle #2 holds all the shapes that have sides all the same length. From the resource page, we have five figures with this characteristic: the regular hexagon, the

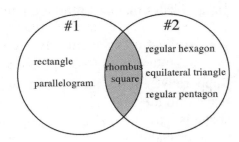

equilateral triangle, the square, the rhombus, and the regular pentagon. All five of these shapes will be completely contained in Circle #2. There are two shapes that are on both lists: the square and the rhombus. These two shapes have all sides the same length **and** they have only two pairs of parallel sides. These two shapes, the square and the rhombus, must be listed in the region that is in both circles, which is shaded above.

Example 2

Based on the markings on each shape below, give the figure the best, most specific name possible.

a)

b)

c)

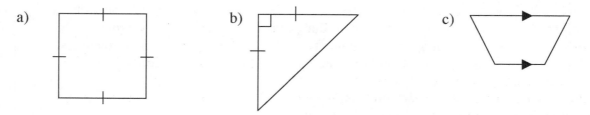

Students created a Shapes Toolkit, that is, a resource page showing many different shapes. Using terms, definitions, and characteristics we have seen, the students named the shapes on the sheet and added appropriate markings. Certain markings mean certain things in geometry. The figure in (a) appears to be a square, but based on the markings, we cannot conclude that. The markings show that the sides of the quadrilateral are equal in length, but equal sides are not enough to make a square. To be a square it would also need right angles. They look like right angles, but maybe they are not quite 90°. Maybe they are 89° and 91°, so without the appropriate markings or other information, we cannot assume the angles are right angles. This quadrilateral with four sides of equal length is called a **rhombus**. Part (b) shows us two types of markings. The small box in the corner of the triangle tells us it is a right angle (measures 90°), so this is a right triangle. We already know that the markings on the sides mean that the sides are the same length. A triangle with two sides that are the same length is called an isosceles triangle. Putting both of these facts together, we can label this figure an **isosceles right triangle**. The arrowheads on the two sides of the quadrilateral of part (c) tells us that those sides are parallel. One pair of parallel sides makes this figure a **trapezoid**.

Example 3

Suppose we cut out the three shapes shown in the last example and place them into a bag. If we reach into the bag and randomly pull out a figure without looking, what is the probability that the shape is a triangle? What is the probability the shape has at least two sides of equal length? What is the probability that the shape has more than four sides?

To calculate probability, we count the number of ways a desired outcome can happen (successes) and divide that by the total number of possible outcomes. This explains why the probability of flipping tails with a fair coin is $\frac{1}{2}$. The number of ways we can get tails is one since there is only one tail, and the total number of outcomes is two (either heads or tails). In our example, to calculate the probability that we pull out a triangle, we need to count the number of triangles in the bag (which is one) and divide that by the total number of shapes in the bag (three). This means the probability that we randomly pull out a triangle is $\frac{1}{3}$. To calculate the probability that we pull out a shape with at least two sides of equal length, we first count the number of shapes that would be a success (i.e., would fit this condition). Both figures in (a) and (b) have at least two sides of equal length, so there are two ways to be successful. When we reach into the bag, there are three possible shapes we could pull out, so the total number of outcomes is three. Therefore, the probability of pulling out a shape with at least two sides of equal length is $\frac{2}{3}$. The probability that we reach into the bag and pull out a shape with more than four sides is done the same way. We know that there are still three outcomes (shapes), so three is still the denominator. But how many ways can we be successful? Are there any shapes with more than four sides? No, so there are zero ways to be successful. Therefore the probability that we pull out a shape with more than four sides is $\frac{0}{3} = 0$.

Problems

Place the shapes from your Shapes Toolkit into the appropriate regions on the Venn Diagram below. The conditions that the shapes must meet to be placed in each circle, #1 and #2, are listed in each problem, Note: each problem, 1 through 3, is separate and will create a new Venn Diagram.

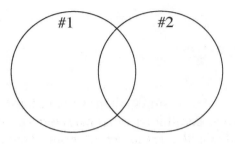

1.   Circle #1: Has more than three sides; Circle #2: Has at least one pair of parallel sides.

2.   Circle #1: Has fewer than four sides; Circle #2: Has at least two sides equal in length.

3.   Circle #1: Has at least one curved side; Circle #2: Has at least one obtuse angle.

Each shape below is missing markings. Add the correct markings so that the shape represents the term listed. Note: the pictures may not be drawn to scale.

4.   A rectangle.

5.   A scalene trapezoid.

6.   An isosceles right triangle.

7.   An equilateral quadrilateral.

Based on the markings, name the figure below with the most specific name. Note: the pictures are not drawn to scale.

8.

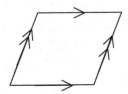

9.

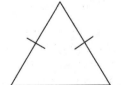

10.

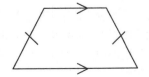

11. On a roulette wheel, there are the numbers 1 through 36 along with 0 and 00. What is the probability that the ball will stop on the number 17?

12. When Davis was finished with his checkers board, he decided to turn it into a dartboard. If he is guaranteed to hit the board, but his dart will hit it randomly, what is the probability he will hit a shaded square?

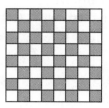

Answers

1. Circle #1 contains: square, rectangle, parallelogram, trapezoid, rhombus, quadrilateral, kite, regular pentagon, and regular hexagon. Circle #2 contains: square, rectangle, parallelogram, trapezoid, rhombus, and regular hexagon. Common to both circles and placed in the overlapping region are: square, rectangle, parallelogram, trapezoid, rhombus, and regular hexagon.

2. Circle #1 contains: equilateral triangle, isosceles triangle, scalene triangle, scalene right triangle, and isosceles right triangle. Circle #2 contains: equilateral triangle, isosceles triangle, isosceles right triangle, square, rectangle, parallelogram, rhombus, kite, regular pentagon, and regular hexagon. Common to both circles and placed in the overlapping region are: equilateral triangle, isosceles triangle, and isosceles right triangle.

3. Circle #1 contains the semicircle and the circle. Circle #2 contains: isosceles right triangle (as pictured), scalene triangle (as pictured), parallelogram, trapezoid, quadrilateral (as pictured), kite, regular pentagon, and regular hexagon. There are no shapes with both characteristics, so there is nothing listed in the overlapping region.

4. A rectangle.

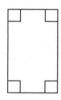

5. A scalene trapezoid.

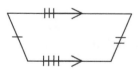

6. An isosceles right triangle.

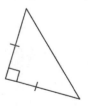

7. An equilateral quadrilateral.

8. A parallelogram

9. An isosceles triangle

10. An isosceles trapezoid

11. $\frac{1}{38}$

12. $\frac{1}{2}$

Applications of geometry in "real world" settings often involve the measures of angles. In this chapter we begin our study of angle measurement. After describing angles and recognizing their characteristics, students complete an Angle Measurement Toolkit. This sheet lists the names of the angles as well as important information about them. The list includes complementary angles (pairs of angles with measures that sum to 90°), supplementary angles (pairs of angles with measures that sum to 180°), vertical angles (which are always equal in measure), straight angle (which equals 180°), corresponding angles, alternate interior angles, and same-side interior angles. See the Methods and Meanings boxes on pages 76 and 91 for further descriptions and pictures.

See the Math Notes boxes on pages 76, 81, 91, and 100.

Example 1

In each figure below, find the measures of angles a, b, and/or c. Justify your answers.

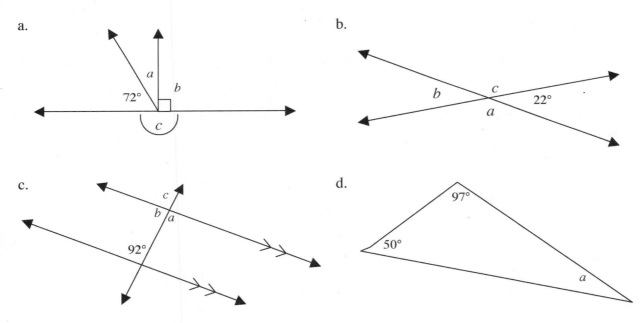

a.

b.

c.

d.

Each figure gives us information that enables us to find the measures of the other angles. In part (a), the little box at angle b tells us that angle b is a right angle, so $m\angle b = 90°$. The angle labeled c is a straight angle (it is opened wide enough to form a straight line) so $m\angle c = 180°$. To calculate $m\angle a$ we need to realize that $\angle a$ and the 72° angle are complementary which means together they sum to 90°. Therefore, $m\angle a + 72° = 90°$ which tells us that $m\angle a = 18°$.

In part (b) we will use two pieces of information, one about supplementary angles and one about vertical angles. First, $m\angle a$ and the 22° angle are supplementary because they form a straight angle (line), so the sum of their measures is 180°. Subtracting from 180° we find that

$m\measuredangle a = 158°$. Vertical angles are formed when two lines intersect. They are the two pairs of angles that are opposite (across from) each other where the lines cross. Their angle measures are always equal. Since the 22° angle and $\angle b$ are a pair of vertical angles, $m\measuredangle b = 22°$. Similarly, $\measuredangle a$ and $\measuredangle c$ are vertical angles, and therefore equal, so $m\measuredangle c = 158°$.

The figure in part (c) shows two parallel lines that are intersected by a transversal. When this happens we have several pairs of angles with equal measures. $\measuredangle a$ and the 92° angle are called alternate interior angles, and since the lines are parallel (that is what the arrows on the lines mean), these angles are equal. Therefore, $m\measuredangle a = 92°$. There are several ways to calculate the remaining angles. One way is to realize that $\measuredangle a$ and $\measuredangle b$ are supplementary. Another uses the fact that $\measuredangle b$ and the 92° angle are same-side interior angles, which makes them supplementary because the lines are parallel. Either way gives the same result: $m\measuredangle b = 180° - 92° = 88°$. There is also more than one way to calculate $m\measuredangle c$. We know that $\measuredangle c$ and $\measuredangle b$ are supplementary. Alternately, $\measuredangle c$ and the 92° angle are corresponding angles which are equal because the lines are parallel. A third way is to see that $\measuredangle c$ and $\measuredangle a$ are vertical angles. With any of these approaches, $m\measuredangle c = 92°$.

Part (d) is a triangle. In class, the students investigated the measures of the angles of a triangle. They found that the sum of the measures of the three angles always equals 180°. Knowing this, we can calculate $m\measuredangle a$: $m\measuredangle a + 50° + 97° = 180°$. Therefore, $m\measuredangle a = 33°$.

Problems

Use what you know about angle measures to find x, y, or z.

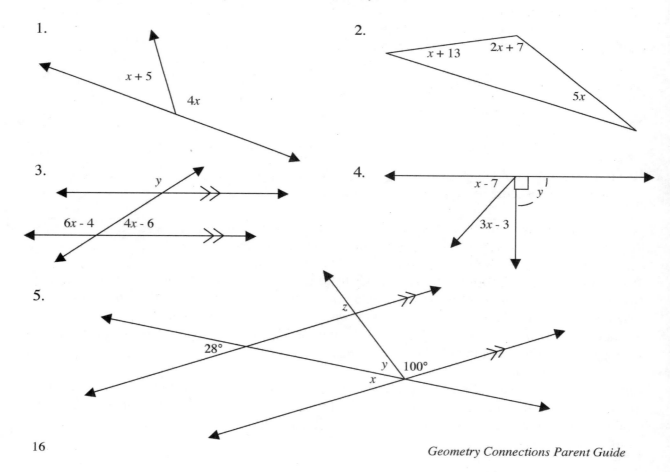

1.

$x + 5$

$4x$

2.

$x + 13$ $2x + 7$

$5x$

3.

y

$6x - 4$ $4x - 6$

4.

$x - 7$

y

$3x - 3$

5.

$28°$

z

y $100°$

x

6.

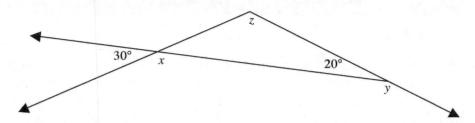

In Lesson 2.1.5 we used what we have learned about angle measures to create proofs by contradiction. (See the Methods and Meanings box on page 186.) Use this method of proof to justify each of your conclusion to problems 7 and 8 below.

7.   Nik scored 40 points lower than Tess on their last math test. The scores could range from 0 to 100 points. Could Tess have scored a 30 on this test? Justify using a proof by contradiction.

8.   Can a triangle have two right angles? Justify your answer with a proof by contradiction.

Answers

1. $(x+5)+4x=180$, $x=35$

2. $(x+13)+(2x+7)+5x=180°$, $x=20$

3. $(6x-4)+(4x-6)=180$, $x=19$, $y=110°$

4. $(x-7)+(3x-3)=90$, $x=25$, $y=90°$

5. $x=28°$, $y=52°$, $z=80°$

6. $x=150°$, $y=160°$, $z=130°$

7. If Tess scored 30 points, then Nik's score would be -10, which is impossible. So Tess cannot have a score of 30 points.

8. If a triangle has two right angles, then the measure of the third angle must be zero. However, this is impossible, so a triangle cannot have two right angles. OR: If a triangle has two 90° angles, the two sides that intersect with the side between them would be parallel and never meet to complete the triangle, as shown in the figure.

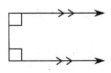

After measuring various angles, students look at measurement in more familiar situations, that of length and area on a flat surface. The students develop methods and formulas for calculating the areas of triangles, parallelograms and trapezoids. They also find the areas of more complicated shapes by partitioning them into shapes for which they can use the basic area formulas. Students also learn how to determine the height of a figure with respect to a particular base.

See the Math Notes box on page 112.

Example 1

In each figure, one side is labeled "base." For this "base," draw in a corresponding height.

a.

base

b.

base

c.

base

d.

base

To find how tall a person is, we have them stand erect and measure the distance from the highest point on their head straight down to the floor. We measure the height of figures in a similar way. One way to visualize height is to imagine that the shape, with its base horizontal, needs to slide into a tunnel. How high must the tunnel be so that the shape will slide into it? The length of the height will answer this. The height, then, is perpendicular to the base (or a line that contains the base) from any of the shape's "highest" point(s). The students also used a 3 x 5 card to help them draw in the height.

a. It is often easier to draw in the height of a figure when the base is horizontal, or the "bottom" of the figure. The height of the triangle below is drawn from the highest point down to the base and forms a right angle with the base.

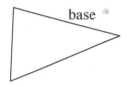

Even though the shape below is not a triangle, it still has a height. In fact, the height can be drawn in any number of places from the side opposite the base. Three heights, all of equal length, are shown.

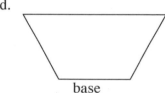

c.   The base of the first triangle below is different from the one in part (a) in that it is not horizontal nor at the bottom. Rotate the shape, then draw the height as we did in part (a).

d.   Shapes like the trapezoid below or the parallelogram in part (b) have at least one pair of parallel sides. Because the base is one of the parallel sides, we can draw several heights. The height at far right below shows a situation where the height is drawn to a line that contains the base segment.

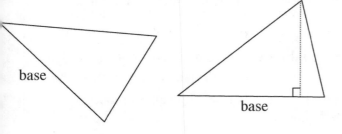

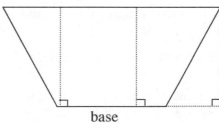

Example 2

Find the area of each shape or its shaded region below. Be sure to include the appropriate units of measurement.

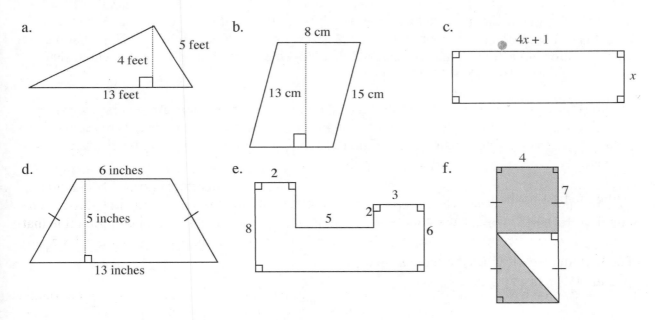

The students have the formulas for the areas of different shapes on their Area Toolkit. For part (a), the area of a triangle is $A = \frac{1}{2}bh$, where b and h are perpendicular to each other. In this case, the base is 13 feet and the height is 4 feet. The side which is 5 feet is not a height because it does not meet the base at a right angle. Therefore, $A = \frac{1}{2}(13)(4) = 26$ square feet. Area is measured in **square** units, while length (such as a perimeter) is measured in linear units, such as feet.

The figure in part (b) is a parallelogram and the area of a parallelogram is $A = bh$ where b and h are perpendicular. Therefore $A = (13)(8) = 104$ square cm.

The figure in part (c) is a rectangle so the area is also $A = bh$, but in this case, we have variable expressions representing the lengths. We still calculate the area in the same way. $A = (4x+1)(x) = 4x^2 + x$ square units. Since we do not know in what units the lengths are measured, we say the area is just "square units."

Part (d) shows a trapezoid; the students found several different ways to calculate its area. The most common way is: $A = \frac{1}{2}(b_1 + b_2)h$ where b_1 is the upper base and b_2 is the lower base. As always, b and h must be perpendicular. The area is $A = \frac{1}{2}(6+13)5 = 47.5$ square inches.

The figures shown in parts (e) and (f) are more complicated and one formula alone will not give us the area. In part (e), there are several ways to divide the area into basic familiar shapes. One way is to divide the figure into three rectangles. The areas of the rectangles on either end are easy to find since the dimensions are labeled on the figure. The area of rectangle (1) is $A = (2)(8) = 16$ square units.

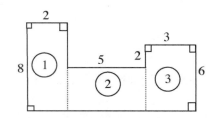

The area of rectangle (3) is $A = (3)(6) = 18$ square units. To find the area of rectangle (2), we have to determine its height. We know the length is 5; the height is 2 shorter than 6, so the height is 4. Therefore, the area of rectangle (2) is $A = (5)(4) = 20$ square units. Now that we know the area of each rectangle, we can add them together to find the area of the whole shape: $A(\text{whole figure}) = 16 + 18 + 20 = 54$ square units.

In part (f), we are finding the area of the shaded region, and again, there are several ways to do this. One way is to see it as the sum of a rectangle and a triangle. Another way is to see the shaded figure as a tall rectangle with a triangle cut out of it. Either way will give the same answer.

Using the first method,
$A = 4(7) + \frac{1}{2}(4)(7) = 42$ square units.

The bottom method gives the same answer:
$A = 4(14) - \frac{1}{2}(4)(7) = 42$ square units.

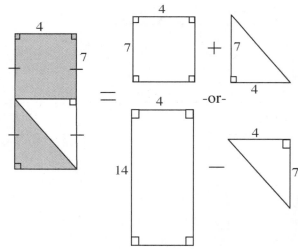

Problems

For each figure below, draw in a corresponding height for the labeled base.

1.

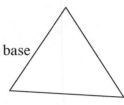

base

2.

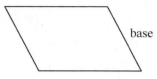

base

3.

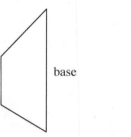

base

4.

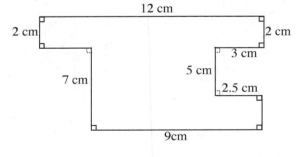

base

Find the area of each shape and/or shaded region. Be sure to include the appropriate units.

5.

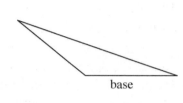

$3x + 5$

$2x$

6.

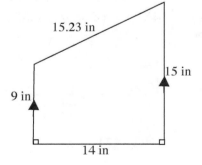

6.2 cm

7.

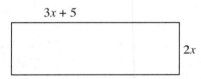

5

12

8.

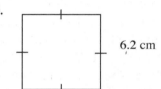

6 in

4 in

15.5 in

9.

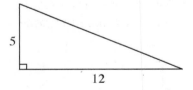

12 cm

2 cm

2 cm

3 cm

5 cm

7 cm

2.5 cm

9cm

10.

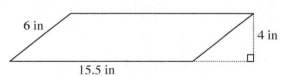

15.23 in

15 in

9 in

14 in

11.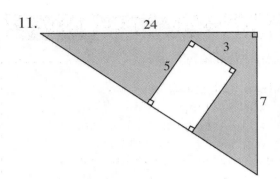

12.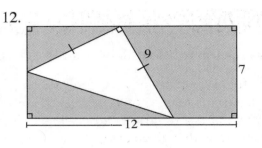

Answers

1.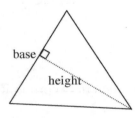

2.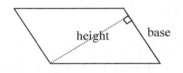

3. Any of these: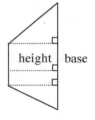

4.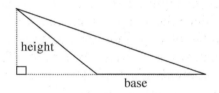

5. $2x(3x+5) = 6x^2 + 10x$ square units

6. $(6.2)^2 = 38.44$ square cm

7. $\frac{1}{2}(12)5 = 30$ square units

8. $(15.5)(4) = 62$ square inches

9. $2(12) + 7(6.5) + 2(2.5) = 74.5$ sq. cm

10. $9(14) + \frac{1}{2}(14)(6) = 168$ square inches

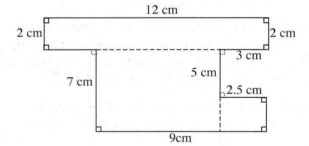

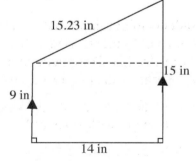

11. $\frac{1}{2}(7)(24) - (3)(5) = 84 - 15 = 69$ square unit

12. $(12)(7) - \frac{1}{2}(9)(9) = 84 - 40.5 = 43.5$ square units

After a reminder of what a "square root" is, the students look at different ways to determine lengths of segments through calculation rather than measurement. They use a method that reinforces the understanding of "square root" (the length of a side of a square with a given area) then use it to apply the Pythagorean Theorem in right triangles. We also study the Triangle Inequality, which determines the restrictions on the possible lengths of the third side of a triangle once we know the lengths of two of its sides.

See the Math Notes Boxes on pages 115, 119, and 123.

Example 1

Name the shape at right. Then calculate the value for x. What do we call this number? Explain.

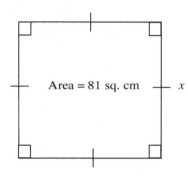

The quadrilateral has four sides of equal length and four right angles. That means the shape is a square. Since the area is 81 sq. cm, we can find the value of x by finding a positive number that, when we multiply it by itself, we get 81. That number is $x = 9$. We say that 9 is the square root of 81 and write $\sqrt{81} = 9$.

Example 2

The triangle at right does not have the lengths of its sides labeled. Can the sides have lengths of:

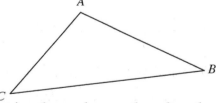

a)   3, 4, 5?   b)   8, 2, 12?

At first, students might think that the lengths of the sides of a triangle can be any three lengths, but that is not so. Students used a dynamic tool to explore the restrictions on the lengths of the sides of a triangle. The Triangle Inequality says that the length of any side must be less than the sum of the lengths of the other two sides. For the triangle in part (a) to exist, all of these statements must be true: $3 + 4 \overset{?}{>} 5$, $4 + 5 \overset{?}{>} 3$, and $5 + 3 \overset{?}{>} 4$. Since each of them is true, we could draw a triangle with sides of lengths 3, 4, and 5. In part (b) we need to check whether $8 + 2 \overset{?}{>} 12$, $2 + 12 \overset{?}{>} 8$, and $12 + 8 \overset{?}{>} 2$. In this case, only two of the three conditions are true, namely, the last two. The first inequality is not true so we cannot draw a triangle with side lengths of 8, 2, and 12. One way to make a convincing argument about this is to cut linguine or coffee stirrers to these lengths and see if you can put the pieces together at their endpoints to form a triangle.

Example 3

Use the Pythagorean Theorem to find the value of x.

a.

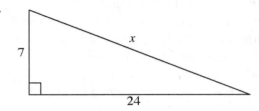

b.

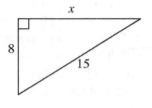

The two sides of a right triangle that form the right angle are called the **legs**, while the third side, the longest side of the triangle, is called the **hypotenuse**. The relationship between the lengths of the legs and the hypotenuse is shown at right.

The Pythagorean Theorem

$$(leg)^2 + (leg)^2 = (hypotenuse)^2$$

In part (a), this gives us:

$$7^2 + 24^2 = x^2$$
$$49 + 576 = x^2$$
$$625 = x^2$$

To find the value of x, use a calculator to find the square root of 625:

$$x = \sqrt{625}, \text{ so } x = 25$$

Part (b) is a bit different in that the variable is not the hypotenuse so the equation is:

$$8^2 + x^2 = 15^2$$
$$64 + x^2 = 225$$
$$x^2 = 225 - 64$$
$$x^2 = 161$$
$$x = \sqrt{161}$$
$$x \approx 12.69$$

Problems

1.   A square has an area of 144 square feet. What is the length of one of its sides?

2.   A square has an area of 484 square inches. What is the length of one of its sides?

3.   A square has an area of 200 square cm. What is the length of one of its sides?

4.   A square has an area of 169 square units. What is the perimeter of the square?

The triangle at right does not have any of the lengths of the sides labeled. Can the triangle have side lengths of:

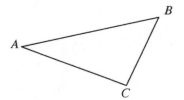

5.   1, 2, 3?

6.   7, 8, 9?

7.   4.5, 2.5, 6?

8.   9.5, 1.25, 11.75?

Use the Pythagorean Theorem to find the value of x. When necessary, round your answer to the nearest hundredth.

9.

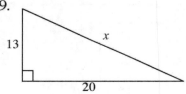

10.

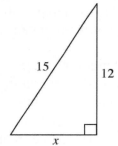

11.

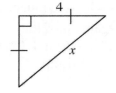

12.

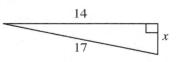

Answers

1.   12 feet

2.   22 inches

3. ≈ 14.14 cm

4.   52 units

5.   No. $1 + 2$ is not greater than 3.

6.   Yes

7.   Yes

8.   No. $9.5 + 1.25$ is not greater than 11.75

9. ≈ 23.85 units

10.   9 units

11. ≈ 5.66 units

12. ≈ 9.64 units

So far, students have measured, described, and transformed geometrical shapes. In this chapter we focus on comparing geometrical shapes. We begin by dilating shapes: enlarging them as one might on a copy machine. When the students compare the original and enlarged shapes closely, they discover that the shape of the figure remains exactly the same (this means the angle measures of the enlarged figure are equal to those in the original), but the size changes (the lengths of the sides increase). Although the size changes, the lengths of the sides have a constant ratio, known as the ratio of similarity or zoom factor.

See the Math Notes boxes on pages 138, 142, 145, and 150.

Example 1

Enlarge the figure at right from the origin by a factor of three.

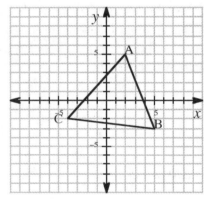

The students used rubber bands to create a dilation (enlargement) of several shapes. We can do this using a grid and slope triangles. Create a right triangle so that the segment from the origin to point A is the hypotenuse, one leg lies on the positive x-axis, and the other connects point A to the endpoint of the leg at $(0, 2)$. This triangle is called a slope triangle since it represents the slope of the hypotenuse from $(0, 0)$ to vertex A. The slope triangle to point A has a vertical leg length of 5 and a horizontal leg length of 2. We will add two more slope triangles exactly like this one along the line from $(0, 0)$ to A as shown in the figure below left. This gives us two new points, $A'(4, 10)$ and $A''(6, 15)$. We do the same thing for the other two vertices, forming a new slope triangle for each vertex. This will give us four more new points

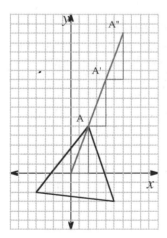

$B'(10, -6)$, $B''(15, -9)$, $C'(-8, -4)$, and $C''(-12, -6)$. If we connect A', B', and C', we form a triangle which is an enlargement of the original figure by a factor of two. If we connect A'', B'', and C'' we form an enlargement which is three times the original figure.

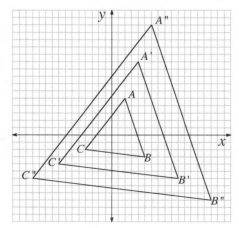

Example 2

The two quadrilaterals at right are similar. What parts are equal? Can you determine the lengths of any other sides?

Similar figures have the same shape, but not the same size. Since the quadrilaterals are similar, we know that all the corresponding angles have the same measure.

This means $m\angle A = m\angle A'$, $m\angle B = m\angle B'$, $m\angle C = m\angle C'$, and $m\angle D = m\angle D'$. In addition, the corresponding sides are **proportional**, which means the ratio of corresponding sides is a constant. To find the ratio, we need to know the lengths of one pair of corresponding sides.

From the picture we see that $\overline{AD}$ corresponds to $\overline{A'D'}$. Since these sides correspond, we can write:

$$\frac{AD}{A'D'} = \frac{4}{6}$$

Therefore, the ratio of similarity is $\frac{4}{6}$, or $\frac{2}{3}$. We can use this value to find the lengths of other sides when we know at least one length of a corresponding pair of sides.

$$\frac{AB}{A'B'} = \frac{4}{6} \qquad\qquad \frac{BC}{B'C'} = \frac{4}{6} \qquad\qquad \frac{CD}{C'D'} = \frac{4}{6}$$
$$\frac{AB}{6} = \frac{4}{6} \qquad\qquad \frac{8}{B'C'} = \frac{4}{6} \qquad\qquad \frac{CD}{12} = \frac{4}{6}$$
$$AB = 4 \qquad\qquad 4B'C' = 48 \qquad\qquad 6CD = 48$$
$$B'C' = 12 \qquad\qquad CD = 8$$

Example 3

The pair of shapes below is similar. Label the second figure correctly to reflect the similarity statement.

ABCDEF ~ UVWXYZ

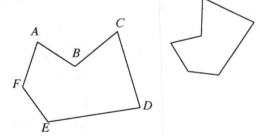

As we have stated, similar figures have the same shape, just different sizes, and this means that the corresponding angles have equal measure. When we write a similarity statement, we write the letters so that the corresponding equal angles match up. By the similarity statement, we must have $m\angle A = m\angle U$, $m\angle B = m\angle V$, $m\angle C = m\angle W$, $m\angle D = m\angle X$, $m\angle E = m\angle Y$, and $m\angle F = m\angle Z$.

The smaller figure is labeled at right. If it difficult to tell which original angle corresponds to its enlargement or reduction, try rotating the figures so they have the same orientation.

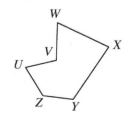

Problems

1. Copy the figure below onto graph paper and then enlarge the shape by a factor of two.

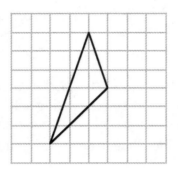

2. Create a figure similar to the one below but with a zoom factor of 0.5.

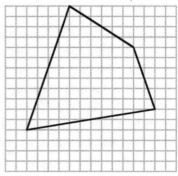

Each pair of figures below is similar. Use what you know about similarity to solve for x.

3.

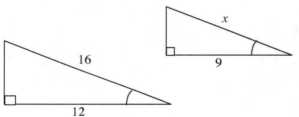

4.

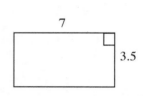

5.

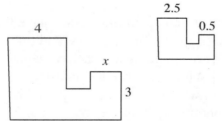

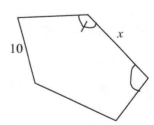

6.

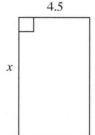

Solve for the missing lengths in the set of similar figures below.

7.   △ABC ~ △PQR

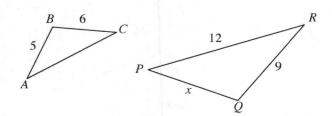

8.   JKLM ~ WXYZ

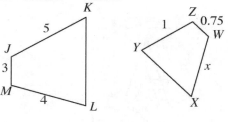

9.   STUV ~ MNOP

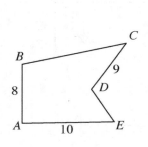
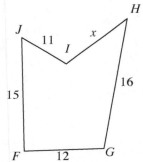

10.   △DAV ~ △ISW

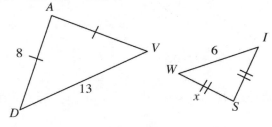

11.   ABCDE ~ FGHIJ

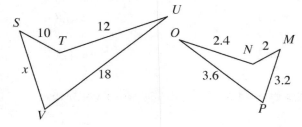

12.   △ABC ~ △DBE

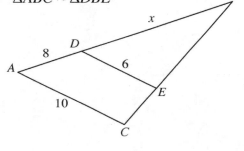

Answers

1.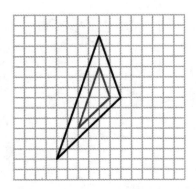

2.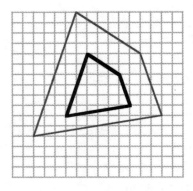

3. $x = 12$

4. $x = 9$

5. $x = 0.8$

6. $x = \frac{40}{3} \approx 13.33$

7. $x = 7.5$

8. $x = 1.25$

9. $x = 16$

10. $x \approx 3.69$

11. $x = 13.5$

12. $x = 12$

Rather than always measuring all the angles and sides of two triangles to check for similarity, in this section the students develop conjectures to shorten the process. These are the **SSS Triangle Similarity Conjecture (SSS~)**, **AA Triangle Similarity Conjecture (AA~)**, and the **SAS Triangle Similarity Conjecture (SAS~)**. The first conjecture states that if all three corresponding side lengths share a common ratio, then the triangles are similar. The second conjecture says if two pairs of corresponding angles have equal measures, then the triangles are similar. The third conjecture says if two pairs of corresponding sides lengths share a common ratio, <u>and</u> the included angles have the same measure, then the triangles are similar. By included angle we mean that the equal angles must be between the two pairs of corresponding sides. Additionally, the students found that if similar figures have a ratio of similarity of one, then the shapes are **congruent**, that is, they have the same size and shape. The students used flow charts in this section to help organize their information and make logical conclusions about similar triangles. Now students are able to use similar triangles to find side lengths, perimeters, heights, and other measurements.

See the Math Notes Boxes on pages 155, 159, 167, and 171.

Example 1

Based on the information given, which pair of triangles is similar? If they are similar, write the similarity statement. Justify your answer completely.

a.
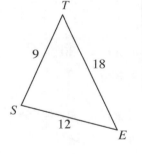

b.
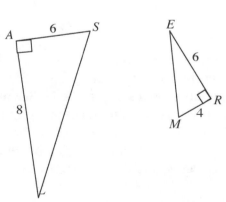

c.
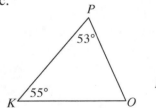

d.
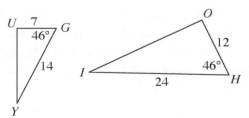

e.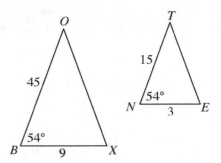

f.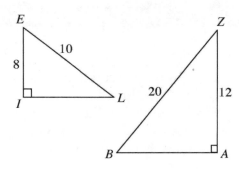

We will use the three conjectures to test whether or not the triangles are similar. In part (a), we have the lengths of the three sides, so it makes sense to check whether the SSS~ holds true. Write the ratios of the corresponding side lengths and compare them to see if each one is the same, as shown at right. Each ratio reduces to 3, so they are equal. Therefore, $\triangle TES \sim \triangle AWK$ by SSS ~.

$$\frac{ST}{KA} \overset{?}{=} \frac{TE}{AW} \overset{?}{=} \frac{ES}{WK}$$

$$\frac{9}{3} = \frac{18}{6} = \frac{12}{4}$$

The measurements given in part (b) suggest we look at SAS ~. $\angle A$ and $\angle R$ are the included angles. Since they are both right angles, they have equal measure. Now we need to check that the corresponding sides lengths have the same ratio, as shown at right.

$$\frac{LA}{ER} \overset{?}{=} \frac{AS}{RM}$$

$$\frac{8}{6} \overset{?}{=} \frac{6}{4}$$

Although the triangles display the SAS~ pattern and the included angles have equal measures, the triangles are not similar because the corresponding side lengths do not have the same ratio.

$$\frac{8}{6} = \frac{4}{3}, \frac{6}{4} = \frac{3}{2}$$

so $\frac{8}{6} \neq \frac{6}{4}$

In part (c), we are given the measures of two angles of each triangle, but not corresponding angles. $\angle K = 55° = \angle N$ which is one pair of corresponding angles, but for AA~, we need two pairs of equal angles. If we use the fact that the measures of the three angles of a triangle add up to 180°, we can find the measures of $\angle O$ and $\angle E$. Now we see that all pairs of corresponding angles have equal measures, so $\triangle POK \sim \triangle EMN$ by AA~.

$$m\angle O = 180° - 53° - 55°$$

$$m\angle O = 72°$$

$$m\angle E = 180° - 55° - 72°$$

$$m\angle E = 53°$$

Part (d) shows the SAS~ pattern and we can see that the included angles have equal measures, $m\angle G = m\angle H$. We also need to have the ratio of the corresponding side lengths to be equal. Since the two fractions are equal (the second reduces to the first), the corresponding side lengths have the same ratio. Therefore, $\triangle YUG \sim \triangle IOH$ by SAS ~.

$$\frac{UG}{OH} \overset{?}{=} \frac{GY}{HI}$$

$$\frac{7}{12} = \frac{14}{24}$$

In part (e), we see that the included angles have equal measures, $m\angle B = m\angle N$. Since $\frac{45}{15} = \frac{9}{3} = \frac{3}{1}$, the corresponding sides are proportional. Therefore, $\triangle BOX \sim \triangle NTE$ by SAS ~.

In part (f), we only have one pair of angles that are equal (the right angles), but those angles are not between the sides with known lengths. However, we can find the length of the third sides by using the Pythagorean Theorem.

$$8^2 + (IL)^2 = 10^2$$
$$64 + (IL)^2 = 100$$
$$(IL)^2 = 36$$
$$IL = 6$$

$$12^2 + (AB)^2 = 20^2$$
$$144 + (AB)^2 = 400$$
$$(AB)^2 = 256$$
$$AB = 16$$

Now that we know all three sides we can check to see if the triangles are similar by SSS ~. Since the ratio of corresponding sides is a constant, $\triangle ELI \sim \triangle BZA$ by SSS~.

$$\frac{12}{6} \overset{?}{=} \frac{16}{8} \overset{?}{=} \frac{20}{10}$$
$$2 = 2 = 2$$

Example 2

In the figure at right, $\overline{AY} \parallel \overline{HP}$. Decide whether or not there are any similar triangles in the figure. Justify your answer with a flow chart. Can you find the length of $\overline{AY}$? If so, find it. Justify your answer.

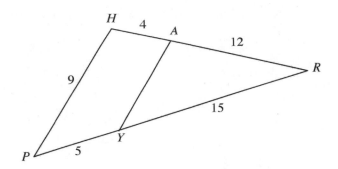

Recalling information we studied in earlier chapters, the parallel lines give us angles with equal measures. In this figure, we have two pairs of corresponding angles with equal measures: $m\angle PHR = m\angle YAR$ and $m\angle HPR = m\angle AYR$. With two pairs of corresponding angles with equal measures, we can say the triangles are similar: $\triangle PHR \sim \triangle YAR$ by AA~. Since the triangles are similar, the lengths of corresponding sides are proportional (i.e., have the same ratio). This means we can write

$$\frac{RA}{RH} = \frac{AY}{HP}$$
$$\frac{12}{16} = \frac{AY}{9}$$
$$AY = \frac{9 \cdot 12}{16} = 6.75$$

We can justify this result with a flowchart as well. The flowchart at right organizes and states what is written above.

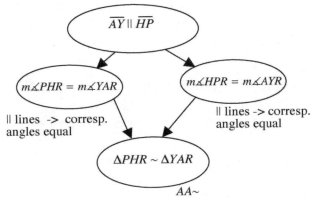

Problems

Each pair of figures below is similar. Write the correct similarity statement and solve for x.

1.

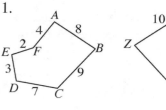
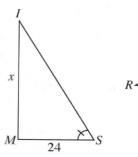

2.

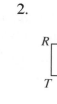
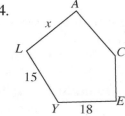
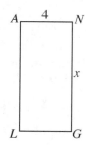

3.

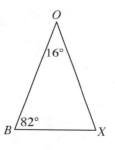

4.

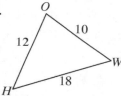
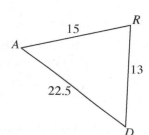

Decide if each pair of triangles is similar. Write a correct similarity statement, and justify your answer.

5.

6.

7.

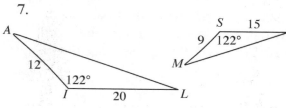

8.

9. In the figure at right $\overline{AB} \parallel \overline{DE}$. Is $\triangle ABC$ similar to $\triangle EDC$? Use a flowchart to organize and justify your answer.

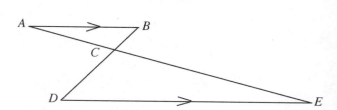

10. Standing four feet from a mirror resting on the flat ground, Palmer, whose eye height is 5 feet, 9 inches, can see the reflection of the top of a tree. He measures the mirror to be 24 feet from the tree. How tall is the tree? Draw a picture to help solve the problem.

34

Answers

1. $ABCDEF \sim UZYXWV$, $x = 3.75$

2. $RECT \sim NGLA$, $x = 8$

3. $\triangle IMS \sim \triangle RCH$, $x = 72$

4. $LACEY \sim ITHOM$, $x = 16.5$

5. $\triangle BOX \sim \triangle NCA$ by $AA\sim$

6. The triangles are not similar because the sides are not proportional.
$\frac{12}{15} = \frac{18}{22.5} = 0.8$, $\frac{10}{13} \approx 0.76$

7. $\triangle ALI \sim \triangle MES$ by SAS $\sim$.

8. The triangles are not similar. On $\triangle SAM$, the 60° is included between the two given sides, but on $\triangle UEL$ the angle is not included.

9.

Note: there is more than one way to solve this problem. Corresponding angles could have been used twice rather than mentioning vertical angles.

10. The figures at right show a sketch of the situation and how it translates into a diagram with triangles. $\triangle PFM \sim \triangle TRM$ by $AA\sim$. The proportion is

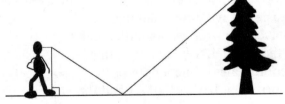

$$\frac{x}{5.75} = \frac{24}{4}$$
$$4x = 138$$
$$x = 34.5$$

Therefore, the tree is 34.5 feet tall.

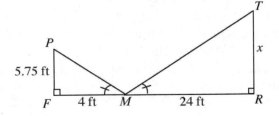

In the first part of Chapter 4, students consider different slope triangles for a given line or segment and notice that on each line, the slope remains constant no matter where they draw the slope triangle on that line or how large or small each slope triangle is. These slope triangles allow students to find lengths of sides and angle measures that they previously could not calculate. This study leads to the **tangent** relationship, the first of the trigonometric functions we will study. Using the tangent function and their calculators, students are able to find measurements in application problems.

See the Math Notes boxes on pages 190, 194, and 200.

Example 1

The line graphed at right passes through the origin. Draw in three different slope triangles. For each triangle, what is the slope ratio, $\frac{\Delta y}{\Delta x}$? What is true about all three ratios?

Note: Δx and Δy are read "change in x" and "change in y."

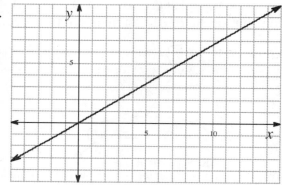

A slope triangle is a right triangle that has its hypotenuse on the line that contains it. This means that the two legs of the right triangle are parallel to the axes: one leg runs vertically, the other horizontally. There are infinitely many slope triangles that we can draw, but it is always easiest if we draw triangles that have their vertices on lattice points (that is, their vertices have integer coordinates). The length of the horizontal leg we call Δx and the length of the vertical leg we call Δy. At right are three possibilities. For the smallest triangle, $\Delta x = 3$ (the length of the horizontal leg), and $\Delta y = 2$ (the length of the vertical leg). For the smallest triangle we have

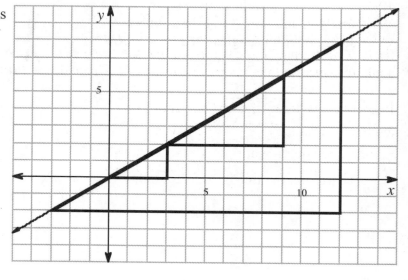

$$\frac{\Delta y}{\Delta x} = \frac{2}{3}.$$

In the medium sized triangle, $\Delta x = 6$ and $\Delta y = 4$, which means:

$$\frac{\Delta y}{\Delta x} = \frac{4}{6}$$

Lastly, we can find the same lengths on the largest triangle: $\Delta x = 15$ and $\Delta y = 10$, so:

$$\frac{\Delta y}{\Delta x} = \frac{10}{15}$$

If we reduce the ratios to their lowest terms we find that the slope ratios, no matter where we draw the slope triangles for this line, are all equal.

$$\frac{\Delta y}{\Delta x} = \frac{2}{3} = \frac{4}{6} = \frac{10}{15}$$

The students also discovered that when the slope of the line (and thus the hypotenuse) changes, the slope ratio changes as well: the steeper the line, the larger the slope ratio, and the flatter the line, the smaller the slope ratio.

Example 2

Using the tangent button on your calculator rather than your Trig Table resource page, find the missing side length in each triangle.

a)

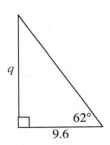

b)

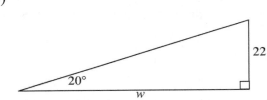

When using the tangent button on a calculator with these problems, you must be sure that the calculator is in degree mode and not radian mode. Your student should be able to check this and fix it, if necessary. Since we found that the slope ratio depends on the angle, we can use the angle measure and the tangent button on the calculator to find unknown lengths of the triangle.

In part (a), we know that the tangent of the angle is the ratio $\frac{opposite\ leg}{adjacent\ leg} = \frac{\Delta y}{\Delta x}$. This allows us to write the equation at right and solve it. We found the value of "tan 62°" on the calculator.

$$\tan 62° = \frac{q}{9.6} \left(\frac{opposite\ leg}{adjacent\ leg} \right)$$
$$9.6(\tan 62°) = q$$
$$q \approx (9.6)(1.88) \approx 18.048$$

In part (b) we will set up another equation similar to the previous one. This equation is slightly different from the one in our first example in that the variable is in the denominator rather than the numerator. This adds another step to the solution process. Some students might realize that they can rotate the triangle and use the 70° angle (which they would have to determine using the sum of the measures of the angles of the triangle) so that the unknown side length is in the numerator.

$$\tan 20° = \frac{22}{w}$$
$$w = \frac{22}{\tan 20°}$$
$$w \approx 60.44$$

Example 3

Talula is standing 117 feet from the base of the Washington Monument in Washington, D.C. She uses her clinometer to measure the angle of elevation to the top of the monument to be 78°. If Talula's eye height is 5 feet, 3 inches, what is the height of the Washington Monument?

With all real world applications, the first step is always the same: draw a picture of what the problem is describing. Here, we have a girl looking up at the top of the monument. We know how far away Talula is standing from the monument, we know her eye height, and we know the angle of elevation of her line of sight.

We translate this information from the picture to a line diagram, as shown at right. On this diagram we include all the measurements we know. Then we write an equation using the tangent function and solve for x.

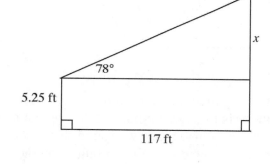

We add the "eye height" to the value of x to find the height of the Washington Monument: $549.9 + 5.25 = 555.15$ feet.

$$\tan 78° = \frac{x}{117}$$
$$117(\tan 78°) = x$$
$$x \approx 549.9 \text{ feet}$$

Problems

For each line, draw in several slope triangles. Calculate the slope ratio.

1.

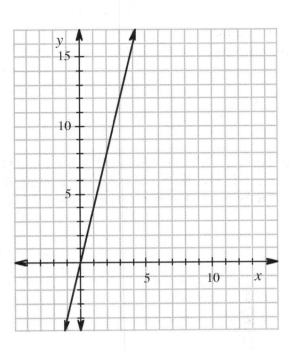

2.

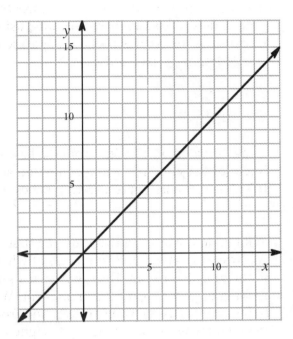

3.

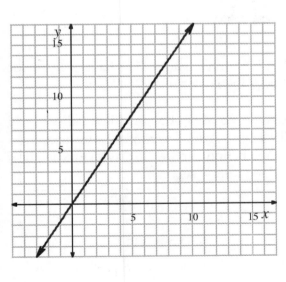

4.

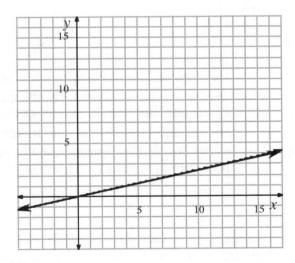

Use the tangent button on your calculator to solve for the variables. It may be helpful to rotate the triangle so that it resembles a slope triangle.

5.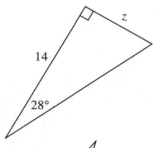

6.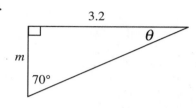

7.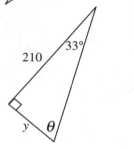

8.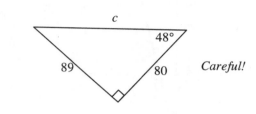

Careful!

9.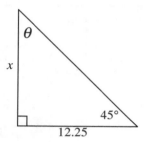

10.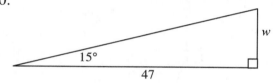

11. A ladder makes a 75° angle with the wall it is leaning against. The base of the ladder is 5 feet from the wall. How high up the wall does the ladder reach?

12. Davis and Tess are 30 feet apart when Tess lets go of her helium-filled balloon, which rises straight up into the air. (It is a windless day.) After 4 seconds, Davis uses his clinometer to site the angle of elevation to the balloon at 35°. If Davis' eye height is 4 feet, 6 inches, what is the height of the balloon after 4 seconds?

Answers

1. In each case the slope ratio is $\frac{4}{1} = 4$.

    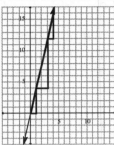

2. The slope ratio is $\frac{5}{5} = \frac{4}{4} = \frac{3}{3} = \frac{1}{1}$.

    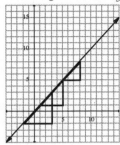

3. The slope ratio is $\frac{5}{3}$.

    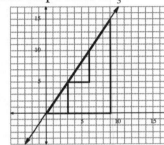

4. The slope ratio is $\frac{1}{4}$.

    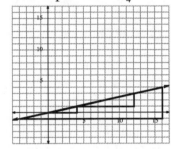

5. $\tan 28° = \frac{z}{14}$, $z \approx 7.44$

6. $\tan 70 = \frac{3.2}{m}$, $m \approx 2.75$, $\theta = 20°$

7. $\tan 33 = \frac{y}{210}$, $y \approx 136.38$, $\theta = 57°$

8. $c \approx 119.67$ (Pythagorean Theorem)

9. $\theta = 45°$, $x = 12.25$

10. $\tan 15° = \frac{w}{47}$, $w \approx 12.59$

    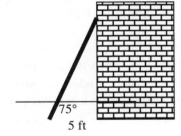

11. $\tan 75° = \frac{h}{5}$; the ladder reaches about 18.66 feet up the wall.

12. $\tan 35° = \frac{h}{30}$, $h \approx 21 + 4.5 \approx 25.5$; at four seconds the balloon is about 25.5 feet above the ground.

Although the definition of probability is simple, calculating a particular probability can be tricky at times. When calculating the probability of flipping a coin and having it come up tails, we can easily see that there are only two possibilities and one successful outcome. But what if neither the total number of outcomes nor the total number of successes is obvious? In this case, we need to have an accurate way to count the number of these events. In these sections of the text, we look at three models to do this: making a systematic list, making a tree diagram, and making an area model. Each different model has its strengths and weakness, and is appropriate in different situations.

See the Math Notes box on page 219.

Example 1

As Ms. Dobby prepares the week's dinner menu for the students, she has certain rules that she must follow. She must have a meat dish and a vegetable at each dinner. She has four choices for her entree: chicken, fish, beef, and pork. Her list of choices for vegetables is a bit larger: peas, carrots, broccoli, corn, potatoes, and turnips. Considering just the meat and the vegetable, what is the probability that the first meal she makes will have meat and a green vegetable?

To determine the probability of a meal of meat and a green vegetable, we need to know how many different meals are possible. Then we need to count how many of the meals have meat and a green vegetable. To count all of the possible meals, we will make a systematic list, pairing each entree with a vegetable in an organized way.

Chicken	Fish	Beef	Pork
Chicken and peas	Fish and peas	Beef and peas	Pork and peas
Chicken and carrots	Fish and carrots	Beef and carrots	Pork and carrots
Chicken and broccoli	Fish and broccoli	Beef and broccoli	Pork and broccoli
Chicken and corn	Fish and corn	Beef and corn	Pork and corn
Chicken and potatoes	Fish and potatoes	Beef and potatoes	Pork and potatoes
Chicken and turnips	Fish and turnips	Beef and turnips	Pork and turnips

From this list we can count the total number of meals: 24 meals. Then we count the number of meals with meat and a green vegetable (peas or broccoli). There are six such meals. Therefore the probability of the first meal having meat and a green vegetable is $\frac{6}{24} = \frac{1}{4}$.

Example 2

What is the probability of flipping a fair coin 4 times and have tails come up exactly two of those times?

To solve this problem, we could make a systematic list as we did with the previous example, but there is another technique that works well with this type of problem. Since each flip gives us only two outcomes, we can organize this information in a tree diagram. The first flip has only two possibilities: heads (H) or tails (T). From each branch, we split again into H or T. We do this for each flip of the coin. The final number of branches at the end tells us the total number of outcomes. In this problem, there are 16 outcomes. We now count the number of "paths" along the branches that have exactly two Ts. One path consisting of HTHT is highlighted. The others are HHTT, HTTH, THHT, THTH, and TTHH, for a total of six paths. Thus the probability of flipping a coin four times and having T come up exactly two times is $\frac{6}{16} = \frac{3}{8}$.

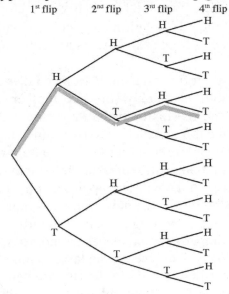

Example 3

Romeo the rat is going to run through a maze to find a block of cheese. The floor plan of the maze is shown at right, with the cheese to be placed in either section A or B. If every time Romeo comes to a split in the maze he is equally like to choose any path in front of him, what is the probability he ends up in section A?

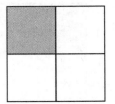

To answer this question we will construct an area model to represent this situation. Using an area model is like turning the problem into a dartboard problem. It is easy to see what the probability of hitting the shaded portion on the dartboard at right is because the shaded portion makes up one-fourth of the board. Therefore the probability of hitting the shaded portion is $\frac{1}{4}$. What we want to do is turn the maze problem into a dartboard with the outcome we want (our success) represented by the shaded part.

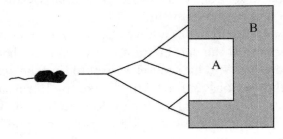

To begin, we start with a square dartboard. You can think of this as being a 1 x 1 square. When Romeo comes to the first branch in the maze, he has two choices: a top path and a bottom path. We represent this on the dartboard by splitting the board into two same sized (equally likely) pieces. Then consider

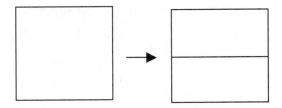

what happens if Romeo chooses the bottom path first. If he chooses the bottom path, he comes to another split with two choices, each equally likely. On the area model (dartboard) we show this by splitting the bottom rectangle into two equally like sections.

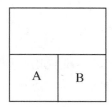

With one branch, Romeo will end up in section A; with the other branch he will end up in B. We indicate this by putting the letters in the regions representing these outcomes. Note: you can split the bottom rectangle in half with a "top" rectangle and a "bottom" rectangle as well. Since we are ultimately going to consider the area covered with an "A," it can be split in any way as long as the pieces are equal in size.

Now consider the top path. If Romeo takes the top path at the first split, he quickly comes to another split where again he has a choice of a top path or a bottom path. Once again we split the top rectangle into two same-sized rectangles since each path is equally likely. One box will represent the top path and one will represent the bottom. If Romeo takes the lower path, he will end up in section A. We indicate this by choosing one of the new regions as representing the lower path, and writing an A in that portion. If Romeo takes the upper path, he comes to another split, each equally likely. This means the last section of the dartboard that is not filled in needs to be cut into two equal parts, since each path is equally likely. One of the paths will lead directly to section A, the other to section B. Now we can fill in those letters as well.

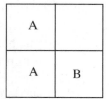

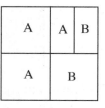

By looking at the dart board now, we can see that since A takes up more of the board, we would be more likely to hit section A. But to find the actual probability, we must determine how much area the sections marked with A take up. Recall that this is a 1×1 square. We can find the fraction of the area of each part. Remember: the key is that we divided regions up into equal parts. The lengths of each side of each rectangle is shown on the exterior of the square, while the area is written within the region. We want to know the probability of getting into section A, which is represented by the shaded portion of the dartboard. The area of the shaded region is

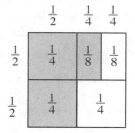

$$A = \tfrac{1}{4} + \tfrac{1}{4} + \tfrac{1}{8}$$
$$= \tfrac{2}{8} + \tfrac{2}{8} + \tfrac{1}{8}$$
$$= \tfrac{5}{8}$$

Therefore the probability of Romeo wandering into section A is $\frac{5}{8}$. This means the probability that he wanders into section B is $\frac{3}{8}$ since the sum of both probabilities must be 1.

Example 4

In the previous problem, if we let Romeo run through the maze randomly 80 times, how many times would you expect him to end up in section A? In section B?

Now that we know the probability of Romeo wandering into each of the sections, we can figure out how many times we would <u>expect</u> him to reach each section. Since the probability of Romeo wandering into section A is $\frac{5}{8}$, we would expect Romeo to end up in section A 50 out of 80 times. Similarly, we would expect Romeo to wander into section B 30 times out of 80. This does not mean that Romeo will definitely wander into A 50 times out of 80. We are dealing with probabilities, not certainties, and this just gives us an idea of what to expect.

Problems

1. If Keisha has four favorite shirts (one blue, one green, one red, and one yellow) and two favorite pairs of pants (one black and one brown), how many different favorite outfits does she have? What is the best way to count this?

2. Each morning Aaron starts his day with either orange juice or apple juice followed by cereal, toast or scrambled eggs. How many different morning meals are possible for Aaron?

3. Eliza likes to make daily events into games of chance. For instance, before she went to buy ice cream at the local ice cream parlor, she created two spinners. The first has her three favorite flavors while the second has "Cone" and "Dish." Eliza will order whatever comes up on the spinners. What is the probability that she will be eating tutti fruitti ice cream from a dish?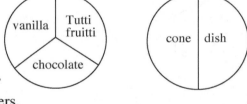

4. Barty is going to flip a coin three times. What is the probability that he will see <u>at least</u> two tails?

5. Mr. Fudge is going to roll two fair dice, one green and one red. What is the probability that the sum will be four or less?

6. Welcome to another new game show, "Spinning for Luck!" As a contestant, you will be spinning two wheels. The first wheel determines a possible dollar amount that you could win. The second wheel is the "multiplier." You will multiply the two results of your spin to determine the amount you will win. Unfortunately, you could <u>owe</u> money if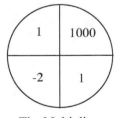

Dollar amount   The Multiplier

your multiplier lands on -2! What is the probability that you could win $100 or more? What is the probability that you could owe $100 or more?

For problems 7-10, a bag contains the figures shown below right. If you reach in and pull out a shape at random, what is the probability that you pull out:

7. a figure with at least one right angle?

8. a figure with an acute angle?

9. a shape with at least one pair of parallel sides?

10. a triangle?

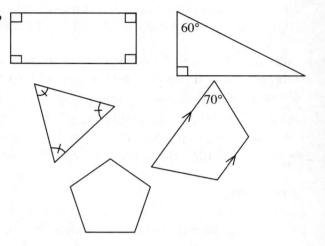

Answers

1. Eight different outfits. A systematic list works best.

2. Six meals. A systematic list or tree diagram works.

3. $\frac{1}{3} \cdot \frac{1}{2} = \frac{1}{6}$ 4. $\frac{1}{2}$ (See the tree diagram in example 2.)   5. $\frac{10}{36} = \frac{5}{18}$

6. Winning \$100 or more: $\frac{5}{12}$, owing \$100 or more: $\frac{1}{12}$

7. $\frac{2}{5}$ 8. $\frac{3}{5}$ 9. $\frac{2}{5}$ 10. $\frac{2}{5}$

We next introduce two more trigonometric ratios: sine and cosine. Both of them are used with acute angles of right triangles, just as the tangent ratio is. Using the diagram below:

$$\sin\theta = \frac{opposite\ leg}{hypotenuse}$$ and from chapter 4:

$$\cos\theta = \frac{adjacent\ leg}{hypotenuse}$$ $$\tan\theta = \frac{opposite\ leg}{adjacent\ leg}$$

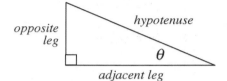

Note: If you decide to use the other acute angle in the triangle, then the names of the legs switch places. The opposite leg is always across the triangle from the acute angle you are using.

See the Math Notes boxes on pages 241 and 248.

Example 1

Use the sine ratio to find the length of the unknown side in each triangle below.

a)

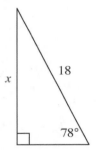

b)

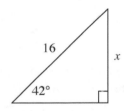

The sine of the angle is the ratio $\frac{opposite\ leg}{hypotenuse}$. For part (a) we will use the 78° as θ. From the 78° angle, we find which side of the triangle is the opposite leg and which side is the hypotenuse. The hypotenuse is always the longest side, and it is always opposite the right angle. In this case, it is 18. From the 78° angle, the opposite leg is the side labeled x. Now we can write the equation at right and solve it.

$$\sin 78° = \frac{x}{18} \ \left(\frac{opposite}{hypotenuse}\right)$$
$$18\sin 78° = x$$
$$x \approx 17.61$$

In part (b), from the 42° angle, the opposite leg is x and the hypotenuse is 16. We can write and solve the equation at right. Note: In most cases, it is most efficient to wait until the equation has been solved for x, then use your calculator to combine the values, as shown in these examples.

$$\sin 42° = \frac{x}{16}$$
$$16(\sin 42°) = x$$
$$x \approx 10.71$$

Example 2

Use the cosine ratio to find the length of the unknown side in each triangle below.

a)

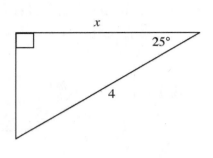

b)

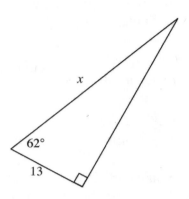

Just as before, we set up an equation using the cosine ratio, $\frac{adjacent\ leg}{hypotenuse}$. Remember that you can always rotate the page, or trace and rotate the triangle, if the figure's orientation is causing confusion. The key to solving these problems is recognizing which side is adjacent, which is opposite, and which is the hypotenuse. (See the box above Example 1 for this information.) For part (a), the angle is 25°, so we can write and solve the equation at right.

$$\cos 25° = \frac{x}{4} \quad \left(\frac{adjacent}{hypotenuse}\right)$$
$$4(\cos 25°) = x$$
$$x \approx 3.63$$

In part (b), from the 62° angle, the adjacent leg is 13 and the hypotenuse is x. This time, our variable will be in the denominator. As we saw in earlier chapters, this will add one more step to the solution.

$$\cos 62° = \frac{13}{x}$$
$$x \cos 62° = 13$$
$$x = \frac{13}{\cos 62°} \approx 27.69$$

Example 3

In each triangle below, use the inverse trigonometry buttons on your calculator to find the measure of the angle θ to the nearest hundredth.

a)

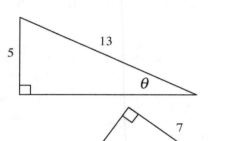

b)

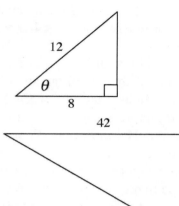

c)

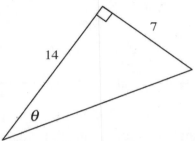

d)

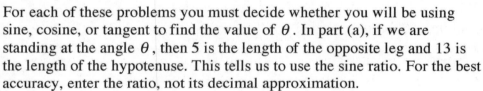

For each of these problems you must decide whether you will be using sine, cosine, or tangent to find the value of θ. In part (a), if we are standing at the angle θ, then 5 is the length of the opposite leg and 13 is the length of the hypotenuse. This tells us to use the sine ratio. For the best accuracy, enter the ratio, not its decimal approximation.

$$\sin\theta = \frac{5}{13}$$
$$\sin\theta \approx 0.385$$

To find the value of θ, find the button on the calculator that says $\sin^{-1}$. (Note: calculator sequences shown are for most graphing calculators. Some calculators use a different order of keystrokes.) This is the "inverse sine" key, and when a ratio is entered, this button tells you the measure of the angle that has that sine ratio. Here we find $\sin^{-1}\frac{5}{13} \approx 22.62°$ by entering "2nd," "sin," $(5 \div 13)$, "enter." Be sure to use parentheses as shown.

In part (b), 8 is the length of the adjacent leg and 12 is the length of the hypotenuse. This combination of sides fits the cosine ratio. We use the $\cos^{-1}$ button to find the measure of θ by entering the following sequence on the calculator: "2nd," "cos," $(8 \div 12)$, "enter."

$$\cos\theta = \frac{8}{12}$$
$$\cos\theta \approx 0.667$$
$$\theta = \cos^{-1}\frac{8}{12}$$
$$\theta \approx 48.19°$$

In part (c), from θ, 7 is the length of the opposite leg and 14 is the length of the adjacent leg. These two sides fit the tangent ratio. As before, you need to find the $\tan^{-1}$ button on the calculator.

$$\tan\theta = \frac{7}{14} = 0.5$$
$$\tan\theta = 0.5$$
$$\theta = \tan^{-1}0.5 \approx 26.57°$$

If we are standing at the angle θ in part (d), 42 is the length of the opposite leg while 30 is the length of the adjacent leg. We will use the tangent ratio to find the value of θ.

$$\tan\theta = \frac{42}{30} = 1.4$$
$$\tan\theta = 1.4$$
$$\theta = \tan^{-1}1.4 \approx 54.46°$$

Example 4

Kennedy is standing on the end of a rope that is 40 feet long and threaded through a pulley. The rope is holding a large metal ball 18 feet above the floor. Kennedy slowly slides her feet closer to the pulley to lower the rod. When the rod hits the floor, what angle (θ) does the rope make with the floor where it is under her foot?

As always, we must draw a picture of this situation to determine what we must do. We start

with a picture of the beginning situation, before Kennedy has started lowering the ball. The second picture shows the situation once the rod has reached the floor. We want to find the angle θ. You should see a right triangle emerging, made of the rope and the floor. The 40 foot rope makes up two sides of the triangle: 18 feet is the length of the leg

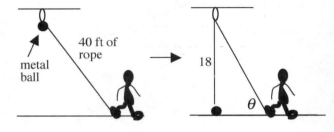

opposite θ, and the rest of the rope, 22 feet of it, is the hypotenuse. With this information, draw one more picture. This one will show the simple triangle that represents this situation.

From θ, we have the lengths of the opposite leg and the hypotenuse. This tells us to use the sine ratio.

$$\sin\theta = \frac{18}{22}$$
$$\theta = \sin^{-1}\frac{18}{22}$$
$$\theta \approx 54.9°$$

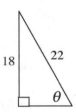

Problems

Using the tangent, sine, and cosine buttons on your calculator, find the value of x to the nearest hundredth.

1.

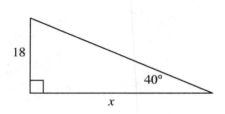

2.

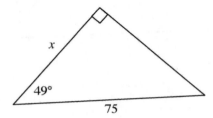

3.

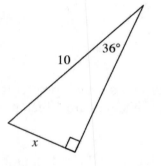

4.

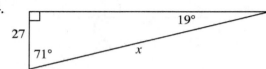

5.

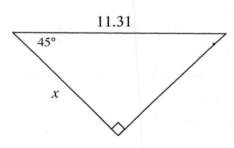

6.

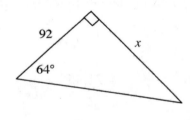

Using the $\sin^{-1}$, $\cos^{-1}$, and $\tan^{-1}$ buttons on your calculator, find the value of θ to the nearest hundredth.

7.

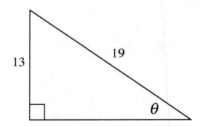

8.

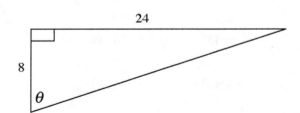

9.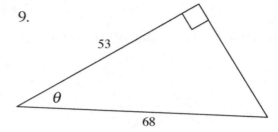

10.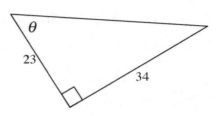

11.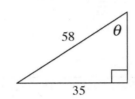

12.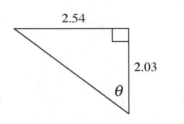

13. Standing 140 feet from the base of a building, Alejandro uses his clinometer to site the top of the building. The reading on his clinometer is 42°. If his eyes are 6 feet above the ground, how tall is the building?

14. An 18 foot ladder rests against a wall. The base of the ladder is 8 feet from the wall. What angle does the ladder make with the ground?

Answers

1. $\tan 40° = \frac{18}{x}$, $x \approx 21.45$

2. $\cos 49° = \frac{x}{75}$, $x \approx 49.20$

3. $\sin 36° = \frac{x}{10}$, $x \approx 5.88$

4. $\sin 19° = \frac{27}{x}$ or $\cos 71° = \frac{27}{x}$, $x \approx 82.93$

5. $\cos 45° = \frac{x}{11.31}$, $x \approx 8.00$

6. $\tan 64° = \frac{x}{92}$, $x \approx 188.63$

7. $\sin \theta = \frac{13}{19}$, $\theta \approx 43.17°$

8. $\tan \theta = \frac{24}{8}$, $\theta \approx 71.57°$

9. $\cos \theta = \frac{53}{68}$, $\theta \approx 38.79°$

10. $\tan \theta = \frac{34}{23}$, $\theta \approx 55.92°$

11. $\sin \theta = \frac{35}{58}$, $\theta \approx 37.12°$

12. $\tan \theta = \frac{2.54}{2.03}$, $\theta \approx 51.37°$

13. $\tan 42° = \frac{h}{140}$, $h \approx 132$ feet

14, $\cos \theta = \frac{8}{18}$, $\theta \approx 63.61°$

There are two special right triangles that occur often in mathematics: the 30°-60°-90° triangle and the 45°-45°-90° triangle. By AA~, all 30°-60°-90° triangles are similar to each other, and all 45°-45°-90° triangles are similar to each other. Consequently, for each type of triangle, the sides are proportional. The sides of these triangles follow these patterns.

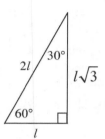

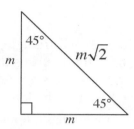

Another short cut in recognizing side lengths of right triangles are Pythagorean Triples. The lengths 3, 4, and 5 are sides of a right triangle (Note: you can verify this with the Pythagorean Theorem) and the sides of all triangles similar to the 3-4-5 triangle will have sides that form Pythagorean Triples (6-8-10, 9-12-15, etc). Another common Pythagorean Triple is 5-12-13.

See the Math Notes boxes on pages 252 and 260.

Example 1

The triangles below are either a 30°-60°-90° triangle or a 45°-45°-90° triangle. Decide which it is and find the lengths of the other two sides based on the pattern for that type of triangle.

a)

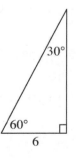

b)

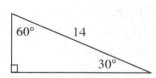

c)

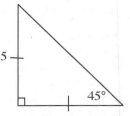

d)

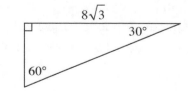

e)

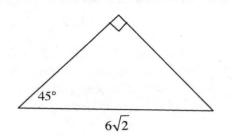

f)

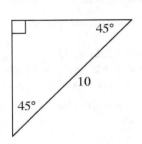

In part (a), this is a 30°-60°-90° triangle, so its sides will fit the pattern for such a triangle. The pattern tells us that the hypotenuse is twice the length of the short leg. Since the short leg has a length of 6, the hypotenuse has a length of 12. The long leg is the length of the short leg times $\sqrt{3}$, so the long leg has a length of $6\sqrt{3}$.

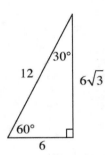

In part (b), we have a 30°-60°-90° triangle again, but this time we know the length of the hypotenuse. Following the pattern, this means the length of the short leg is half the hypotenuse: 7. As before, we multiply the length of the short leg by $\sqrt{3}$ to get the length of the long leg: $7\sqrt{3}$.

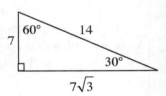

The triangle in part (c) is a 45°-45°-90° triangle. The missing angle is also 45°; you can verify this by remembering the sum of the angles of a triangle is 180°. The legs of a 45°-45°-90° triangle are equal in length (it is isosceles) so the length of the missing leg is also 5. To find the length of the hypotenuse, we multiply the leg's length by $\sqrt{2}$. Therefore the hypotenuse has length $5\sqrt{2}$.

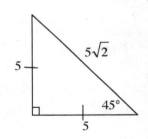

We have another 30°-60°-90° triangle in part (d). This time we are given the length of the long leg. To find the short leg, we <u>divide</u> the length of the long leg by $\sqrt{3}$. Therefore, the length of the short leg is 8. To find the length of the hypotenuse, we double the length of the short leg, so the hypotenuse is 16.

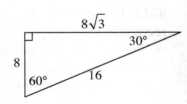

The triangle in part (e) is a 45°-45°-90° triangle, and we are given the length of the hypotenuse. To find the length of the legs (which are equal in length), we will divide the length of the hypotenuse by $\sqrt{2}$. Therefore, each leg has length 6.

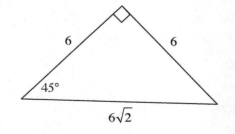

If you understand what was done in each of the previous parts, part (f) is no different from the rest. This is a $45° - 45° - 90°$ triangle, and we are given the length of the hypotenuse. However, we are used to seeing the hypotenuse of a $45° - 45° - 90°$ triangle with a $\sqrt{2}$ attached to it. In the last part when we were given the length of the hypotenuse, we divided by $\sqrt{2}$ to find the length of the legs, and this time we do the same thing.

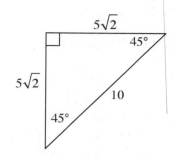

$$\tfrac{10}{\sqrt{2}} = \tfrac{10}{\sqrt{2}} \cdot \tfrac{\sqrt{2}}{\sqrt{2}} = \tfrac{10\sqrt{2}}{2} = 5\sqrt{2}$$

Note: Multiplying by $\frac{\sqrt{2}}{\sqrt{2}}$ is called rationalizing the denominator. It is a technique to remove the radical from the denominator.

Example 2

Use what you know about Pythagorean Triples and similar triangles to fill in the missing lengths of sides below.

a)

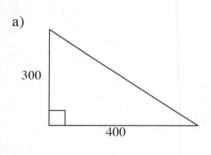

b)

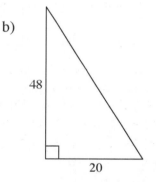

c)

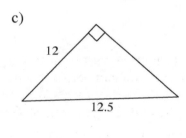

There are a few common Pythagorean Triples that students should recognize; 3–4–5, 5–12–13, 8–15–17, and 7–24–25 are the most common. If you forget about a particular triple or do not recognize one, you can always find the unknown side by using the Pythagorean Theorem if two of the sides are given. In part (a), this is a multiple of a 3–4–5 triangle. Therefore the length of the hypotenuse is 500. In part (b), we might notice that each leg has a length that is a multiply of four. Knowing this, we can rewrite them as $48 = 4(12)$, and $20 = (4)(5)$. This is a multiple of a 5–12–13 triangle, the multiplier being 4. Therefore, the length of the hypotenuse is $4(13) = 52$. In part (c), do not let the decimal bother you. In fact, since we are working with Pythagorean Triples and their multiples, double both sides to create a similar triangle. This eliminates the decimal. That makes the leg 24 and the hypotenuse 25. Now we recognize the triple as 7–24-25. Since the multiple is 0.5, the length of the other leg is 3.5.

Problems

Identify the special triangle relationships. Then solve for x, y, or both.

1.

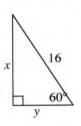

2.

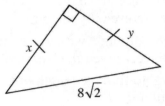

3.

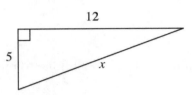

4.

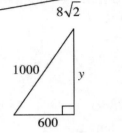

5.

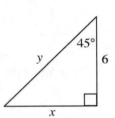

6.

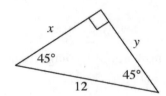

7.

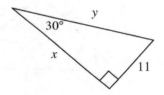

8.

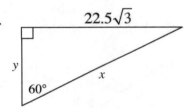

9.

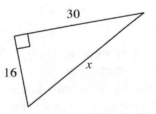

10.

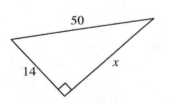

Answers

1. $x = 8\sqrt{3}$, $y = 8$

2. $x = y = 8$

3. $x = 13$

4. $y = 800$

5. $x = 6$, $y = 6\sqrt{2}$

6. $x = y = \frac{12}{\sqrt{2}} = 6\sqrt{2}$

7. $x = 11\sqrt{3}$, $y = 22$

8. $y = 22.5$, $x = 45$

9. $x = 34$

10. $x = 48$

Students have several tools for finding parts of right triangles, including the Pythagorean Theorem, the tangent ratio, the sine ratio, and the cosine ratio. These relationships only work, however, with <u>right</u> triangles. What if the triangle is not a right triangle? Can we still calculate lengths and angles with trigonometry from certain pieces of information? Yes, by using two laws, the Law of Sines and the Law of Cosines that state:

Law of Sines

$$\frac{\sin(m\angle A)}{a} = \frac{\sin(m\angle B)}{b}$$

$$\frac{\sin(m\angle B)}{b} = \frac{\sin(m\angle C)}{c}$$

$$\frac{\sin(m\angle A)}{a} = \frac{\sin(m\angle C)}{c}$$

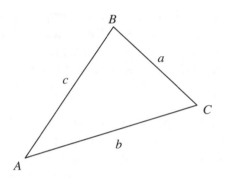

Law of Cosines

$$c^2 = a^2 + b^2 - 2ab\cos C \qquad b^2 = a^2 + c^2 - 2ac\cos B \qquad a^2 = b^2 + c^2 - 2bc\cos A$$

See the Math Notes boxes on pages 264 and 267.

Example 1

Using the Law of Sines, calculate the value of x.

a)

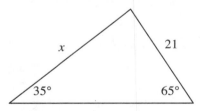

b)

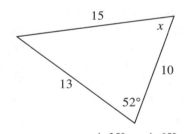

We will set up ratios that are equal according to the Law of Sines. The ratio compares the sine of the measure of an angle to the length of the side opposite that angle. In part (a), 21 is the length of the side opposite the 35° angle, while x is the length of the side opposite the 65° angle. The proportion is shown at right. To solve the proportion, we cross multiply, and solve for x. We can use the Law of Sines to find the measure of an angle as well. In part (b), we again write a proportion using the Law of Sines.

$$\frac{\sin 35°}{21} = \frac{\sin 65°}{x}$$

$$x\sin 35° = 21\sin 65°$$

$$x = \frac{21\sin 65°}{\sin 35°}$$

$$x \approx 33.18$$

$$\frac{\sin x}{13} = \frac{\sin 52°}{15}$$

$$15\sin x = 13\sin 52°$$

$$\sin x = \frac{13\sin 52°}{15}$$

$$\sin^{-1} x = 13\sin 52° \div 15$$

$$x \approx 43.07°$$

Example 2

Use the Law of Cosines to solve for x in the triangles below.

a)

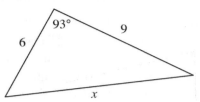

b)

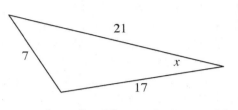

The Law of Cosines does not use ratios, as the Law of Sines does. Rather, it uses a formula somewhat similar to the Pythagorean Theorem. For part (a) the formula gives us the equation and solution shown at right.

$$x^2 = 6^2 + 9^2 - 2(6)(9)\cos 93°$$
$$x^2 \approx 36 + 81 - 108(-0.052)$$
$$x^2 \approx 117 + 5.612$$
$$x^2 \approx 122.612$$
$$x \approx 11.07$$

Just as with the Law of Sines, we can use the Law of Cosines to find the measures of angles as well as side lengths. In part (b) we will use the Law of Cosines to find the measure of angle x. From the law we can write the equation and solution shown at right.

$$7^2 = 17^2 + 21^2 - 2(17)(21)\cos x$$
$$49 = 289 + 441 - 714\cos x$$
$$49 = 730 - 714\cos x$$
$$-681 = -714\cos x$$
$$\frac{-681}{-714} = \cos x$$
$$x \approx 17.49° \text{ (using } \cos^{-1} x)$$

Example 3

Marisa's, June's, and Daniel's houses form a triangle. The distance between June's and Daniel's houses is 1.2 km. Standing at June's house, the angle formed by looking out to Daniel's house and then to Marisa's house is 63°. Standing at Daniel's house, the angle formed by looking out to June's house and then to Marisa's house is 75°. What is the distance between all of the houses?

The trigonometry ratios and laws are very powerful tools in real world situations. As with any application, the first step is to draw a picture of the situation. We know the three homes form a triangle, so we start with that. We already know one distance: the distance from June's house to Daniel's house. We write 1.2 as the length of the side from D to J. We also know that $m\angle J = 63°$ and $m\angle D = 75°$, and can figure out that $m\angle M = 42°$. We are trying to find the lengths of $\overline{DM}$ and $\overline{MJ}$. To do this, we will use the Law of Sines.

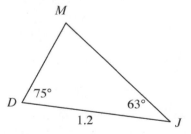

MJ:

$$\frac{\sin 75°}{MJ} = \frac{\sin 42°}{1.2}$$
$$1.2\sin 75° = (MJ)\sin 42°$$
$$\frac{1.2\sin 75°}{\sin 42°} = MJ$$
$$MJ \approx 1.73 \text{ km}$$

MD:

$$\frac{\sin 63°}{DM} = \frac{\sin 42°}{1.2}$$
$$1.2\sin 63° = (DM)\sin 42°$$
$$\frac{1.2\sin 63°}{\sin 42°} = DM$$
$$DM \approx 1.60 \text{ km}$$

Therefore the distances between the homes are: From Marisa's to Daniel's: 1.6 km, from Marisa's to June's: 1.73 km, and from Daniel's to June's: 1.2 km.

Problems

Use the tools you have for triangles to solve for *x*, *y*, or θ.

1.

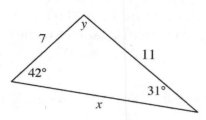

2.

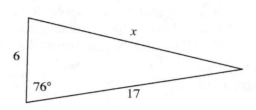

3.

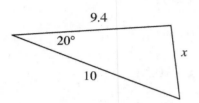

4.

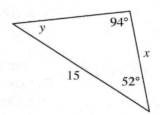

5.

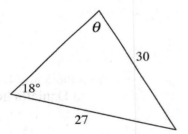

6.

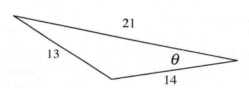

7.

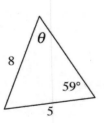

8.

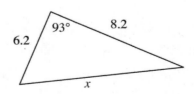

9.

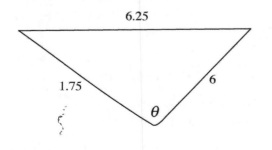

10.

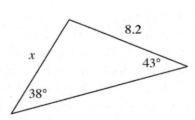

11. Marco wants to cut a sheet of plywood to fit over the top of his triangular sandbox. One angle measures 38°, and it is between sides with lengths 14 feet and 18 feet. What is the length of the third side?

12. From the planet Xentar, Dweeble can see the stars Quazam and Plibit. The angle between these two sites is 22°. Dweeble knows that Quazam and Plibit are 93,000,000 miles apart. He also knows that when standing on Plibit, the angle made from Quazam to Xentar is 39°. How far is Xentar from Quazam?

Answers

1. $x \approx 13.00$, $y = 107°$

2. $x \approx 16.60$

3. $x \approx 3.42$

4. $x \approx 8.41$, $y = 34°$

5. $\theta \approx 16.15°$

6. $\theta \approx 37.26°$

7. $\theta \approx 32.39°$

8. $x \approx 9.08$

9. $\theta = 81.61°$

10. $x \approx 10.54$

11. ≈ 11.08 feet

12. $\approx 156{,}235{,}361$ miles

Sometimes the information we know about sides and angle of a triangle is not enough to make one unique triangle. Sometimes a triangle may not even exist, as we saw when we studied the Triangle Inequality. When a triangle formed is not unique (that is, more than one triangle can be made with the given conditions) we call this **triangle ambiguity**. This happens when we are given two sides and an angle <u>not</u> between the two sides, known as SSA.

Example 1

In $\triangle ABC$, $m\angle A = 50°$, $AB = 12$, and $BC = 10$. Can you make a unique triangle? If so, find all the angle measures and side lengths for $\triangle ABC$. If not, show more than one triangle that meets these conditions.

As with many problems, we will first make a sketch of what the problem is describing.

Once we label the figure, we see that the information displays the SSA pattern mentioned above. It does seem as if this triangle can exist. First try to find the length of side AC. To do this we will use the Law of Cosines.

$$10^2 = 12^2 + x^2 - 2(12)(x)\cos 50°$$
$$100 = 144 + x^2 - 24x\cos 50°$$
$$100 \approx 144 + x^2 - 15.43x$$
$$x^2 - 15.43x + 44 \approx 0$$

Now we have a type of equation we have not seen when solving this sort of problem. This is a quadratic equation. To solve it, we will use the Quadratic Formula. (See the Math Notes box on page 163 for a Quadratic Formula refresher.) Recall that a quadratic equation may have two different solutions. We will use the formula and see what happens.

$$x^2 - 15.43x + 44 = 0$$
$$x = \frac{15.43 \pm \sqrt{15.43^2 - 4(1)(44)}}{2(1)}$$
$$\approx \frac{15.43 \pm \sqrt{238.08 - 176}}{2}$$
$$\approx \frac{15.43 \pm \sqrt{62.08}}{2}$$
$$\approx \frac{15.43 \pm \sqrt{62.08}}{2}$$
$$\approx \frac{15.43 \pm 7.88}{2}$$

Both of these answers are positive numbers, and could be lengths of sides of a triangle. So what happened? If we drew the triangle to scale, we would notice that although we drew the triangle with $\angle C$ acute, it does not have to be. Nothing in the information given says to draw the triangle this way. In fact, since there are no conditions on $m\angle B$ the side $\overline{BC}$ can swing as if it is on a hinge

$$x \approx \frac{15.43 + 7.88}{2} \text{ and } x \approx \frac{15.43 - 7.88}{2}$$
$$x \approx 11.65 \text{ and } x \approx 3.78$$

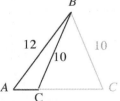 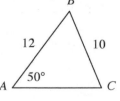

at B. As you move $\overline{BC}$ along $\overline{AC}$, $\overline{BC}$ can intersect $\overline{AC}$ at two different places and still be 10 units long. In one arrangement, $\angle C$ is fairly small while in the second, $\angle C$ is larger. (Note: the triangle formed with the two possible arrangements (the light grey triangle) is isosceles. From that you can conclude that the two possibilities for $\angle C$ are supplementary.)

Problems

Partial information is given about a triangle in each problem below. Solve for the remaining parts of the triangle, explain why a triangle does not exist, or explain why there is more than one possible triangle.

1. In $\triangle ABC$, $\angle A = 32°$, $AB = 20$, and $BC = 12$.

2. In $\triangle XYZ$, $\angle Z = 84°$, $XZ = 6$, and $YZ = 9$.

3. In $\triangle ABC$, $m\angle A = m\angle B = 45°$, and $AB = 7$.

4. In $\triangle PQR$, $PQ = 15$, $\angle R = 28°$, and $PR = 23$.

5. In $\triangle XYZ$, $\angle X = 59°$, $XY = 18$, and $YZ = 10$.

6. In $\triangle PQR$, $\angle P = 54°$, $\angle R = 36°$, and $PQ = 6$.

Answers

1. Two triangles: $AC \approx 22.58$, $m\angle B \approx 85.34°$, $m\angle C \approx 62.66°$ or $AC \approx 11.35$, $m\angle B \approx 30.04°$, $m\angle C \approx 117.96°$.

2. One triangle: $XY \approx 10.28$, $m\angle X \approx 60.54°$, $m\angle Y \approx 35.46°$

3. One triangle: $m\angle C = 90°$, $BC = AC = \frac{7\sqrt{2}}{2} \approx 4.95$

4. Two triangles: $QR \approx 30.725$, $m\angle Q \approx 46.04°$, $m\angle P \approx 105.96°$, or $QR \approx 9.895$, $m\angle Q \approx 133.96°$, $m\angle P \approx 18.04°$.

5. No triangle exists. Note: if you use Law of Cosines, you will have a negative number under the square root sign. This means there are no real number solutions.

6. One triangle: $m\angle Q = 90°$, $QR \approx 8.26$, $PR \approx 10.21$.

Congruent triangles are similar figures with a ratio of similarity of 1, that is $\frac{1}{1}$. One way to prove triangles congruent is to prove they are similar first, and then prove that the ratio of similarity is 1. In these sections of the text the students find short cuts that enable them to prove triangles congruent in fewer steps, by developing five triangle congruence conjectures. They are SSS $\cong$, ASA $\cong$, AAS $\cong$, SAS $\cong$, and HL $\cong$, illustrated below.

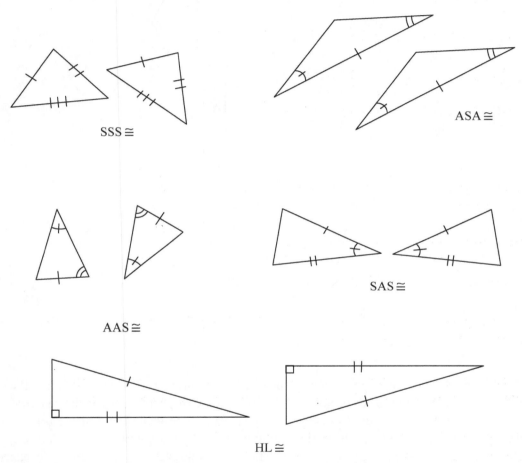

Note: "S" stands for "side" and "A" stands for "angle." HL $\cong$ is only used with right triangles. The "H" stands for "hypotenuse" and the "L" stands for "leg." The pattern appears to be "SSA" but this arrangement is NOT one of our conjectures, since it is only true for right triangles.

See the Math Notes boxes on pages 291 and 299.

Example 1

Use your triangle congruence conjectures to decide whether or not each pair of triangles must be congruent. Base each decision on the markings, not on appearances. Justify each answer.

a)

b)

c)

d)

e)

f)

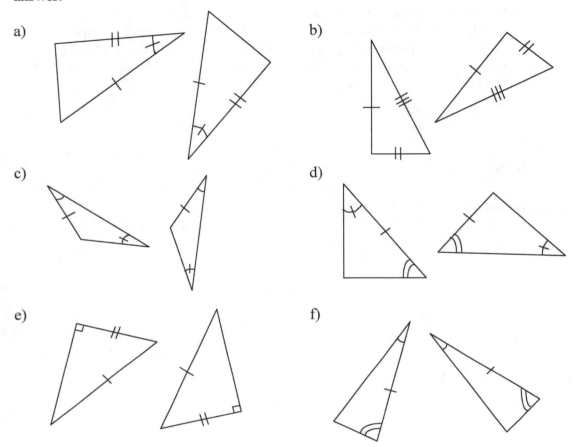

In part (a), the triangles are congruent by the SAS≅ conjecture. The triangles are also congruent in part (b), this time by the SSS≅ conjecture. In part (c), the triangles are congruent by the AAS≅ conjecture. Part (d) shows a pair of triangles that are not necessarily congruent. The first triangle displays an ASA arrangement, while the second triangle displays an AAS arrangement. The triangles could still be congruent, but based on the markings, we cannot conclude that they definitely are congruent. The triangles in part (e) are right triangles and the markings fit the HL≅ conjecture. Lastly, in part (f), the triangles are congruent by the ASA≅ conjecture.

Example 2

Using the information given in the diagrams below, decide if any triangles are congruent, similar but not congruent, or not similar. If you claim the triangles are congruent or similar, create a flow chart justifying your answer.

a)

b)

In part (a), $\triangle ABD \cong \triangle CBD$ by the SAS$\cong$ conjecture. Note: if you only see "SA," observe that $\overline{BD}$ is congruent to itself. The **Reflexive Property** justifies stating that something is equal or congruent to itself.

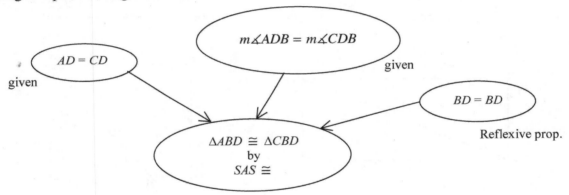

In part (b), $\triangle WXV \sim \triangle ZYV$ by the AA~ conjecture. The triangles are not necessarily congruent; they could be congruent, but since we only have information about angles, we cannot conclude anything else.

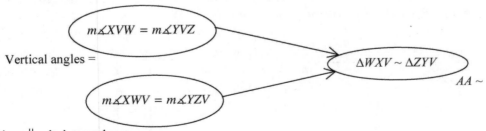

There is more than one way to justify the answer to part (b). There is another pair of alternate interior angles ($\angle WXV$ and $\angle ZYV$) that are equal that we could have used rather than the vertical angles, or we could have used them along with the vertical angles.

Problems

Use your triangle congruence conjectures to decide whether or not the pair of triangles must be congruent. Base your decision on the markings, not on appearances. Justify your answer.

1.
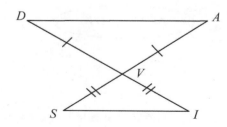

2.
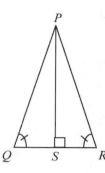

3.
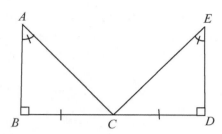

4.
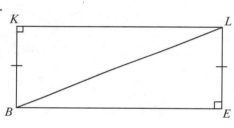

5.
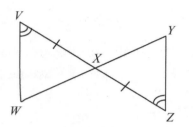

6.
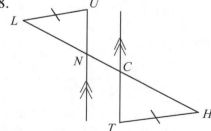

Using the information given in each diagram below, decide if any triangles are congruent, similar but not congruent, or not similar. If you claim the triangles are congruent or similar, create a flow chart justifying your answer.

7.
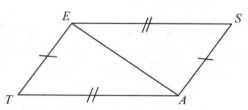

8.
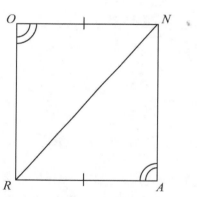

9.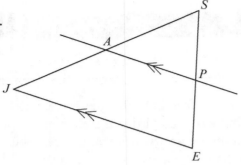

10.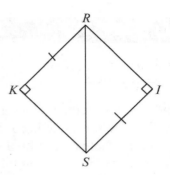

Answers

1. $\triangle ABC \cong \triangle EDC$ by AAS $\cong$

2. $\triangle PQS \cong \triangle PRS$ by AAS $\cong$, with $\overline{PS} \cong \overline{PS}$ by the Reflexive Property.

3. $\triangle VXW \cong \triangle ZXY$ by ASA $\cong$, with $\angle VXW \cong \angle ZXY$ because vertical angles are $\cong$.

4. $\triangle TEA \cong \triangle SAE$ by SSS $\cong$, with $\overline{EA} \cong \overline{EA}$ by the Reflexive Property.

5. $\triangle KLB \cong \triangle EBL$ by HL $\cong$, with $\overline{BL} \cong \overline{BL}$ by the Reflexive Property.

6. Not necessarily congruent.

7. $\triangle DAV \sim \triangle ISV$ by SAS~

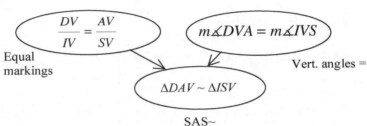

8. $\triangle LUN$ and $\triangle HTC$ are not necessarily similar based on the markings.

9. $\triangle SAP \sim \triangle SJE$ by AA~.

10. $\triangle KRS \cong \triangle ISR$ by HL$\cong$

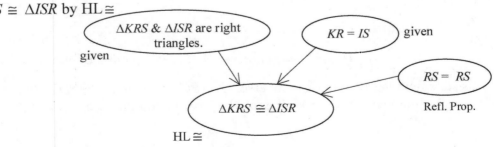

A conditional statement is a sentence in the "If – then" form. "If all sides are equal in length, then a triangle is equilateral" is an example of a conditional statement. We can abbreviate conditional statements by creating an **arrow diagram**. When the clause after the "if" in a conditional statement exchanges places with the clause after the "then," the new statement is called the **converse** of the original. If the conditional statement is true, the converse is not necessarily true, and vice versa.

See the Math Notes box on page 304.

Example 1

Read each conditional statement below. Rewrite it as an arrow diagram, and state whether or not it is true. Then write the converse of the statement, and state whether or not the converse is true.

a)   If a triangle is equilateral, then it is equiangular.

b)   If $x = 4$, then $x^2 = 16$.

c)   If $ABCD$ is a square, then $ABCD$ is a parallelogram.

The arrow diagram for part (a) is not much shorter than the original statement:

$$\Delta \text{ is equilateral} \longrightarrow \Delta \text{ is equiangular}$$

The converse is: If a triangle is equiangular, then it is equilateral. This statement and the original conditional statement are both true.

In part (b), the conditional statement is true and the arrow diagram is:

$$x = 4 \longrightarrow x^2 = 16.$$

The converse of this statement, "If $x^2 = 16$, then $x = 4$," is not necessarily true because x could equal -4.

In part (c), the arrow diagram is:

$$ABCD \text{ is a square} \longrightarrow ABCD \text{ is a parallelogram.}$$

This statement is true, but the converse, "If $ABCD$ is a parallelogram, then $ABCD$ is a square," is not necessarily true. It could be a parallelogram or a rectangle.

Problems

Rewrite each conditional statement below as an arrow diagram and state whether or not it is true. Then write the converse of the statement and state whether or not the converse is true.

1.   If an angle is a straight angle, then the angle measures 180°.

2.   If a triangle is a right triangle, then the sum of the squares of the lengths of the legs is equal to the square of the length of the hypotenuse.

3.   If the measures of two angles of one triangle are equal to the measures of two angles of another triangle, then the measures of the third angles are also equal.

4.   If one angle of a quadrilateral is a right angle, then the quadrilateral is a rectangle.

5.   If two angles of a triangle have equal measures, then the two sides of the triangle opposite those angles have equal length.

Answers

1.   Conditional: true.

   →   180°

Converse: If an angle measures 180°, then it is a straight angle. True.

2.   Conditional: true.

   → $a^2 + b^2 = c^2$

Converse: If the sum of the squares of the lengths of the legs is equal to the square of the length of the hypotenuse, then the triangle is a right triangle. True.

3.   Conditional: true.

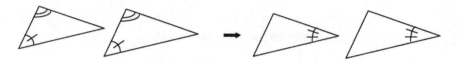

Converse: If the measures of one pair of corresponding angles of two triangles are equal, then the measures of the two other pairs of corresponding angles are also equal. False.

4.   Conditional: false.

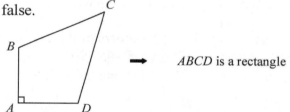   →   ABCD is a rectangle

Converse: If a quadrilateral is a rectangle, then one angle is a right angle. True, in fact, all four angles are right angles.

5.   Conditional: true.

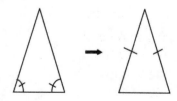

Converse: If two sides of a triangle are equal in length, then the two angles opposite those sides are equal in measure. True.

The remaining sections of Chapter 6 are devoted to doing big problems. The students solve problems that involve many of the topics that they have studied so far, giving them the chance to connect the ideas and information as well as extend it to new situations.

Example 1

To frame a doorway, strips of wood surround the opening creating a "frame." If the doorway's dimensions are 30 inches by 80 inches and the strips of wood are $2\frac{1}{2}$ inches wide, how much wood is needed to frame the doorway and how should it be cut? Assume that the strips will be assembled as shown in the figure at right and that they are sold in 8' lengths.

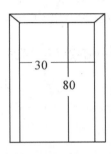

Cutting two pieces of wood 80 inches long, and one piece 30 inches long will not enable us to make a frame for the doorway. The inside edges of the strips of wood will have those measurements, but the outside dimensions of the wood are longer.

The wood strips will meet at a 45° angle at the corners of the doorframe. Looking at the corner carefully (as shown at right) we see two 45°-45°-90° triangles in the corner. The lengths AD and CD are both $2\frac{1}{2}$ inches, since they are the width of the strips of wood.

Since a 45°-45°-90° triangle is isosceles, this means AB and BC are also $2\frac{1}{2}$ inches in length. Therefore, we need two strips that are $82\frac{1}{2}$ inches long ($80 + 2\frac{1}{2}$), and one strip that is 35 inches long ($30 + 2\frac{1}{2} + 2\frac{1}{2}$), because each end must extend the width of the vertical strip). Since the strips come in 8-foot lengths, we would need to buy three of them. Two will be cut at a 45° angle, with the outsides edge $82\frac{1}{2}$ inches long and the inside edges 80 inches long. The third piece has two 45° angle cuts. The outside length is 35 inches while the inside length is 30 inches.

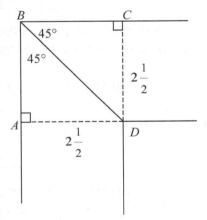

Example 2

A friend offers to play a new game with you, using the spinner shown at right. Your friend says that you can choose to be player 1 or 2. On each turn, you will spin the spinner twice. If the letters are the same, player 1 gets a point. If the letters are different, then player 2 gets the point. Which player would you choose to be? Justify your answer.

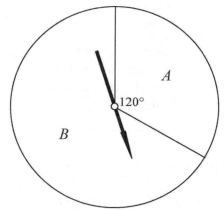

To help us decide which player to be, we will create an area model to represent the probabilities. On the area model, the left edge represents the two outcomes from the first spin; the top edge represents the outcomes from the second spin. On the first spin, there are two possible outcomes, A and B, which are <u>not</u> equally likely. In fact, the probability of B occurring is $P(B) = \frac{2}{3}$, while the probability of A occurring is $P(A) = \frac{1}{3}$. This is true for the first spin and the second spin. We divide the area model according to these probabilities, and fill in the possible outcomes.

Player 1 receives a point when the letters are the same for both spins. This outcome is represented by the shaded squares. Player 2 receives the point when the letters are different. By multiplying the dimensions of each region, the areas are expressed as ninths and we see that:

$$P(1 \text{ gets a point}) = \tfrac{1}{9} + \tfrac{4}{9} = \tfrac{5}{9}$$

and

$$P(2 \text{ gets a point}) = \tfrac{2}{9} + \tfrac{2}{9} = \tfrac{4}{9}$$

	$P(A)=\frac{1}{3}$	$P(B)=\frac{2}{3}$
$P(A)=\frac{1}{3}$	$P(AA)=\frac{1}{9}$	$P(AB)=\frac{2}{9}$
$P(B)=\frac{1}{3}$	$P(BA)=\frac{2}{9}$	$P(BB)=\frac{4}{9}$

Since the probability that player 1 will win a point is greater than the probability that player 2 will, we should choose to be player 1.

Problems

1. On graph paper, plot the points *A*(3, -4), *B*(8, -1), *C*(2, 9), and *D*(-3, 6) and connect them in order. Find all the measurements of this shape (side lengths, perimeter, area, and angle measures) and based on that information, decide the most specific name for this shape. Justify your answer.

2. The spinner at right is only partially completed. Complete the spinner based on these clues.

    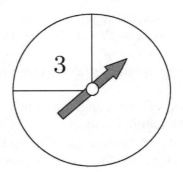

    1) There are three other single digit numbers on the spinner. All four numbers on the spinner are equally likely results for one spin. No digit is repeated.

    2) If the spinner is spun twice and the two outcomes are added, the largest possible sum is 16, while the smallest possible sum is 2. The most common sum is 9.

3. To go along with the snowflakes you are making for the winter dance decorating committee, you are going to make some "Star Polygons." A Star Polygon is formed by connecting equally spaced points on a circle in a specific order from a specified starting point.

    For instance, the circle at right has five equally spaced points. If we connect them in order, the shape is a regular pentagon (dashed sides). But if we connect every other point, continuing until we reach the point that we started with, we get a star.

    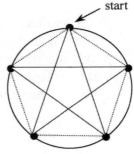

    a) What happens when 6 points are equally spaced around a circle? Under what conditions will you get a "normal" polygon, and when will you get a "star polygon"?

    b) Explore other options. Come up with a rule that explains when a normal polygon is formed when connecting points, and when a star polygon is formed. Consider various numbers of points.

    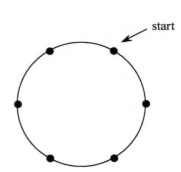

Answers

1. The side lengths are: $AB = CD = \sqrt{34} \approx 5.83$ units,
$AD = CB = \sqrt{136} = 2\sqrt{34} \approx 11.66$ units. Perimeter $= 6\sqrt{34} \approx 34.99$ units. The slope of AB = the slope of CD $= \frac{3}{5}$, slope of AD = slope of CB $= \frac{-5}{3}$. Since the slopes are negative reciprocals, we know that the segments are perpendicular, so all four angles are 90°, so the figure is a rectangle. Area = 68 square units.

2. The spinner is divided into four equal pieces, with the numbers 3, 1, 6, and 8.

3. (a) Connecting consecutive points forms a hexagon. Connecting every other point forms an equilateral triangle. Connecting every third point forms several line segments (diameters), but no star.

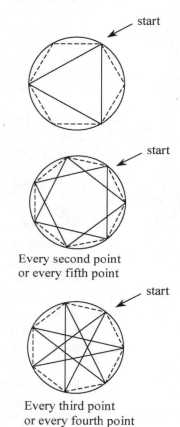

start

start

Every second point
or every fifth point

start

(b) Trying the same things with 7 points around a circle produces more interesting results. Connecting each point in order forms a heptagon (7-gon). Connecting every second point or every fifth point produces the first star polygon at right. Connecting every third point or every fourth point produces the second star polygon at right.

To generalize, if the number of points around the circle is n, and we connect to the rth point, the polygon is a star polygon if n and r have no common factors. Note that whenever r = 1 or r = n – 1, the result is always a polygon.

Every third point
or every fourth point

Circles have special properties. The fact that they can roll smoothly is because the circle has a constant **diameter** (the distance across the circle that passes through the center). A vehicle with square wheels would cause it to bump up and down because, since the diagonals of a square are longer then its width, it does not have a constant diameter. But a circle is not the only shape with a constant diameter. Reuleaux curves, which resemble rounded polygons, also have a constant diameter. It may not appear to be the case, but Reuleaux curves roll smoothly without bumping up and down. See page 337 in the textbook for a picture.

A circle does not include its interior. It is the set of points on a flat surfaceat a fixed distance (the radius) from a fixed point (the center). This also means the **center** of the circle is not part of the circle, nor are the diameters and radii (plural of radius). Remember: a radius is half of a diameter, connecting the center of the circle to a point on the circle. A circle has infinitely many diameters and infinitely many radii.

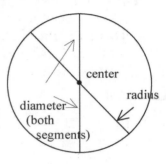

See the Math Notes box on page 341.

Example 1

Using the circle at right, write an equation and solve for x. Note: each part is a different problem.

a) $AO = 3x - 4$, $OB = 4x - 12$.

b) $OB = 2x - 5$, $AC = x - 7$

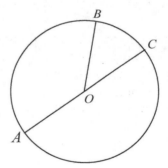

Using the information we have about circles, diameters, and radii, we can write an equation using the expressions in part (a), then solve for x. $\overline{AO}$ and $\overline{OB}$ are both radii of circle O, which means that they are equal in length.

$$AO = OB$$
$$3x - 4 = 4x - 12 \quad \text{Subtract } 3x \text{ and add 12 on both sides.}$$
$$8 = x$$

In part (b), $\overline{OB}$ is a radius, but $\overline{AC}$ is a diameter, so $\overline{AC}$ is twice as long as $\overline{OB}$.

$$2(OB) = AC$$
$$2(2x - 5) = x - 7$$
$$4x - 10 = x - 7$$
$$3x = 3$$
$$x = 1$$

Problems

Using the circle at right, write an equation and solve for x. Note: each part is a different problem.

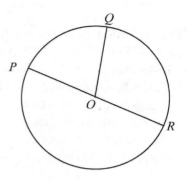

1. $OP = 5x - 3, OR = 3x + 9$

2. $OQ = 2x + 12, OP = 3x - 1$

3. $OR = 12x - 8, OQ = 8x - 4$

4. $OP = 5x + 3, PR = 3x + 13$

5. $OQ = x - 6, PR = x + 7$

Answers

1. $x = 6$

2. $x = 13$

3. $x = 1$

4. $x = 1$

5. $x = 19$

Through the use of transformations (rotations, reflections, etc), students created new figures and discovered properties of these figures. Students also used transformations to discover the shortest path from one object to another (an optimization problem), and to define and study **regular polygons**. A regular polygon is a polygon in which all sides are equal length and all angles have equal measure.

See the Math Notes boxes on pages 346 and 351.

Example 1

On a recent scout camping trip, Zevel was walking back to camp when he noticed that the campfire had grown too large. He wants to fill his bucket at the river, then walk to the fire to douse the flames. To ensure the fire does not get out of control, Zevel wants to take the shortest path. What is the shortest path from where Zevel is standing to go to the river and then to the fire?

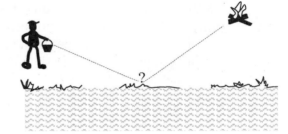

The shortest distance between two points on a flat surface is a straight line. How can we find the shortest distance if a third point is involved, such as Zevel's trip to the river? We use reflections to find the point at the river to which Zevel should walk. Reflecting across a line gives a new figure that is the same distance from the line as the original. Reflecting point F across the river line gives F' with $FX = F'X$. To find the shortest distance from Z to F' we connect them. Since $\angle FXR$ is a right angle, $\triangle FXR \cong \triangle F'XR$ by the SAS$\cong$ conjecture. This means that $FR = F'R$. Since the shortest path from Z to F' is the straight line drawn, then the shortest path from Zevel to the river and then to the fire is to walk from Z to R and then to F.

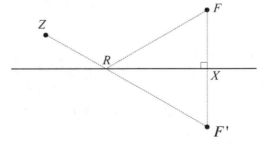

Example 2

If a hinged mirror is set at 10° and the core region is isosceles, how many sides would there be on the polygon that would be reflected in the mirror?

If the core region (the region the hinged mirror encloses on the paper) is isosceles, the reflected image will be a regular polygon. In a regular polygon, all the interior angles are equal in measure and, if the center is connected to each vertex of the polygon, these central angles are equal. If one central angle measures 10° and there are 360° around the center, there are 360° ÷ 10° = 36 sides on the polygon.

Problems

1.   Venetia wants to install two lights in her garden. Each one will be connected to a control timer that will turn the lights on and off automatically. She can mount the timer anywhere on her house, but she wants to minimize the amount of wire she will use. If the wire must run from the light at point *P* to the timer, and then back out to the light at point *Q*, where should Venetia place the timer?

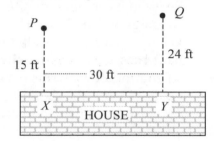

2.   While playing miniature golf last weekend, Myrtle came to the fifth hole and saw that it was a par 1 hole. This meant that she should be able to putt the ball into the hole with one stroke. Explain to Myrtle how knowledge of "shortest distance" problems can help her make the putt.

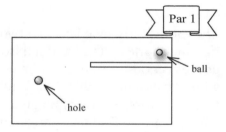

3.   If the center of a regular dodecagon (12 sides) is connected to each vertex of the figure, what is the measure of each angle at the center?

4.   If a central angle of a regular polygon measures 18°, how many sides does the polygon have?

5.   The center point of a regular pentagon is connected to each vertex forming five congruent isosceles triangles. Find the measure of each base angle in the isosceles triangles and use that result to find the measure of one interior angle of the pentagon.

Answers

1.   Venetia should place the timer about 11.54 feet from the point X or 18.45 feet from the point Y on the diagram above.

2.   If Myrtle can aim correctly and hit a straight shot, she can make a hole in one. She can imagine the hole reflected across the top boundary to find the direction to aim. If she hits the wall at the point X, the ball will travel to the hole.

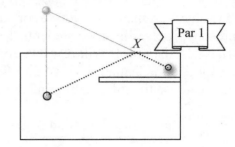

3.   30°

4.   20 sides

5.   Each base angle measures 54°. Two together makes one interior angle of the pentagon, so an interior angle measures 108°.

By tracing and reflecting triangles to form quadrilaterals, the students discover properties about quadrilaterals. More importantly, though, they develop a method to prove that what they have observed is true. Since students are already familiar with flowcharts from earlier work to organize information, they will use flowcharts to present proofs. Since the students developed their conjectures by reflecting triangles, the proofs will rely heavily on the triangle congruence conjectures developed in Chapter 6. Once the students prove that their observations are true, they can use the information in later problems.

See the Math Notes boxes on pages 354, 361, 364, 371, 400, and 464.

Example 1

ABCD at right is a parallelogram. Use this fact and other properties and conjectures to prove that:

a)   the opposite sides are congruent.

b)   the opposite angles are congruent.

c)   the diagonals bisect each other.

Because *ABCD* is a parallelogram, the opposite sides are parallel. Whenever we have parallel lines, we should be looking for some pairs of congruent angles. In this case, since $AB \parallel CD$, $\angle BAC \cong \angle DCA$ because alternate interior angles are congruent. Similarly, since $AD \parallel CB$, $\angle DAC \cong \angle BCA$. Also, $\overline{AC} \cong \overline{CA}$ by the Reflexive Property. Putting all three of these pieces of information

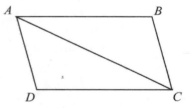

together tells us that $\triangle BAC \cong \triangle DCA$ by the ASA$\cong$ conjecture. Now that we know that the triangles are congruent, all the other corresponding parts are also congruent. In particular, $\overline{AB} \cong \overline{CD}$ and $\overline{AD} \cong \overline{CB}$, which proves that the opposite sides are congruent. As a flowchart proof, this argument would be presented as shown below.

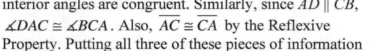

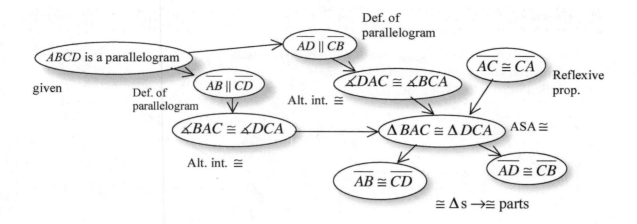

For part (b), we can continue the previous proof, again using congruent parts of congruent triangles, to justify that $\angle ADC \cong \angle CBA$. That gives one pair of opposite angles congruent. To get the other pair, we need to draw in the other diagonal. As before, the alternate interior angles are congruent, $\angle ADB \cong \angle CBD$ and $\angle ABD \cong \angle CDB$, because the opposite sides are parallel. Using the Reflexive Property, $\overline{BD} \cong \overline{BD}$. Therefore, $\triangle ABD \cong \triangle CDB$ by the ASA$\cong$ conjecture. Now that we know that the triangles are congruent, we can conclude that the corresponding parts are also congruent. Therefore, $\angle DAB \cong \angle BCD$. We have just proven that the opposite angles in the parallelogram are congruent.

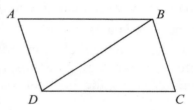

Lastly, we will prove that the diagonals bisect each other. To begin, we need a picture with both diagonals included. There are many triangles in the figure now, so our first task will be deciding which ones we should prove congruent to help us with the diagonals. To show that the diagonals bisect each other we will show that $\overline{AE} \cong \overline{CE}$ and $\overline{BE} \cong \overline{DE}$ since "bisect" means to cut into two equal parts.

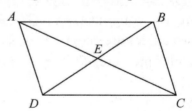

We have already proven facts about the parallelogram that we can use here. For instance, we know that the opposite sides are congruent, so $\overline{AD} \cong \overline{CB}$. We already know that the alternate interior angles are congruent, so $\angle ADE \cong \angle CBE$ and $\angle DAE \cong \angle BCE$. Once again we have congruent triangles: $\triangle ADE \cong \triangle CBE$ by ASA$\cong$. Since congruent triangles give us congruent corresponding parts, $\overline{AE} \cong \overline{CE}$ and $\overline{BE} \cong \overline{DE}$, which means the diagonals bisect each other.

Example 2

PQRS at right is a rhombus. Do the diagonals bisect each other? Justify your answer. Are the diagonals perpendicular? Justify your answer.

The definition of a rhombus is a quadrilateral with four sides of equal length. Therefore, $\overline{PQ} \cong \overline{QR} \cong \overline{RS} \cong \overline{SP}$. By the Reflexive Property, $\overline{PR} \cong \overline{RP}$. With sides congruent, we can use the SSS$\cong$ conjecture to write $\triangle SPR \cong \triangle QRP$. Since the triangles are congruent, all corresponding parts are also congruent. Therefore, $\measuredangle SPR \cong \measuredangle QRP$ and $\measuredangle PRS \cong \measuredangle RPQ$. The first pair of congruent angles means that $\overline{SP} \parallel \overline{QR}$. (If the alternate interior angles are congruent, the lines are parallel.) Similarly, the second pair of congruent angles means that $\overline{PQ} \parallel \overline{RS}$. With both pairs of opposite sides congruent, this rhombus is a parallelogram. Since it is a parallelogram, we can use what we have already proven about parallelograms, namely, that the diagonals bisect each other. Therefore, the answer is yes, the diagonals bisect each other.

To determine if the diagonals are perpendicular, use what we did to answer the first question. Then gather more information to prove that other triangles are congruent. In particular, since $\overline{PQ} \cong \overline{RQ}$, $\overline{QT} \cong \overline{QT}$, and $\overline{PT} \cong \overline{RT}$ (since the diagonal is bisected), $\triangle QPT \cong \triangle RQT$ by SSS $\cong$. Because the triangles are congruent, all corresponding parts are also congruent, so $\measuredangle QTP \cong \measuredangle QTR$. These two angles also form a straight angle. If two angles are congruent and their measures sum to 180°, each angle measures 90°. If the angles measure 90°, the lines must be perpendicular. Therefore, $\overline{QS} \perp \overline{PR}$.

Example 3

In the figure at right, If $\overline{AI}$ is the perpendicular bisector of $\overline{DV}$, is $\triangle DAV$ isosceles? Prove your conclusion using the two-column proof format.

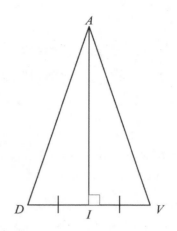

Before starting a two-column proof, it is helpful to think about what we are trying to prove. If we want to prove that a triangle is isosceles, then we must show that $\overline{DA} \cong \overline{VA}$ because an isosceles triangle has two sides congruent. By showing that $\triangle AID \cong \triangle AIV$, we will know that this pair of sides are congruent. Now that we have a plan, we can begin the two-column proof.

Statements	Reason (This statement is true because …)
$\overline{AI}$ is the perpendicular bisector of $\overline{DV}$	Given
$\overline{DI} \cong \overline{VI}$	Definition of bisector
$\angle DIA$ and $\angle VIA$ are right angles	Definition of perpendicular
$\angle DIA \cong \angle VIA$	All right angles are congruent
$\overline{AI} \cong \overline{AI}$	Reflexive Property of Equality
$\triangle DAI \cong \triangle VAI$	SAS $\cong$
$\overline{DA} \cong \overline{VA}$	$\cong \triangle s \rightarrow \cong$ parts
$\triangle DAV$ is isosceles	Definition of isosceles

Problems

1. If $\overline{PQ} \cong \overline{RS}$ and $\overline{QR} \cong \overline{SP}$, is $PQRS$ a parallelogram? Prove your answer.

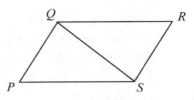

2. $WXYZ$ is a rhombus. Does $\overline{WY}$ bisect $\angle ZWX$? Prove your answer.

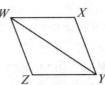

For problems 3 – 5, use the figure at right. Base your decision on the markings, not appearances.

3. Is $\triangle BCD \cong \triangle EDC$? Prove your answer.

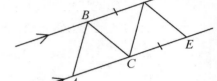

4. Is $\overline{AB} \cong \overline{ED}$? Prove your answer.

5. Is $\overline{AB} \cong \overline{DC}$? Prove your answer.

6. If $MIFH$ is a parallelogram, is $\overline{ES} \cong \overline{ET}$? Prove your answer.

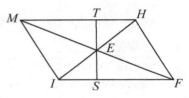

7. If $DSIA$ is a parallelogram and $\overline{IA} \cong \overline{IV}$, is $\angle D \cong \angle V$? Prove your answer.

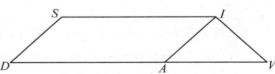

8. If A, W, and K are midpoints of $\overline{TS}$, $\overline{SE}$, and $\overline{ET}$ respectively, is $TAWK$ a parallelogram? Prove your answer.

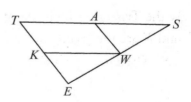

Answers

1.   Yes. $\overline{QS} \cong \overline{SQ}$ (reflexive). This fact, along with the given information means that $\triangle PQS \cong \triangle RSQ$ (SSS$\cong$). That tells us the corresponding parts are also congruent, so $\measuredangle PQS \cong \measuredangle RSQ$ and $\measuredangle PSQ \cong \measuredangle RQS$. These angles are alternate interior angles, so both pairs of opposite sides are parallel. Therefore, $PQRS$ is a parallelogram.

2.   Yes. Since the figure is as a rhombus, all the sides are congruent. In particular, $\overline{WZ} \cong \overline{WX}$ and $\overline{ZY} \cong \overline{XY}$. Also, $\overline{WY} \cong \overline{WY}$ (reflexive), so $\triangle WZY \cong \triangle WXY$ (SSS$\cong$). Congruent triangles give us congruent parts so $\measuredangle ZWY \cong \measuredangle XWY$. Therefore, $\overline{WY}$ bisects $\measuredangle ZWX$.

3.   Yes. Since the lines are parallel, alternate interior angles are congruent so $\measuredangle BDC \cong \measuredangle ECD$. Also, $\overline{DC} \cong \overline{CD}$ (reflexive) so the triangles are congruent by SAS$\cong$.

4.   Not necessarily, since we have no information about $\overline{AC}$.

5.   Not necessarily.

6.   Yes. Because $MIFH$ is a parallelogram, we know several things. First, $\measuredangle TME \cong \measuredangle SFE$ (alternate interior angles) and $\overline{ME} \cong \overline{EF}$ (diagonals of a parallelogram bisect each other). Also, $\measuredangle TEM \cong \measuredangle SEF$ because vertical angles are congruent. This gives us $\triangle MTE \cong \triangle FSE$ by ASA$\cong$. Therefore, the corresponding parts of the triangle are congruent, so $\overline{ES} \cong \overline{ET}$.

7.   Since $DSIA$ is a parallelogram, $\overline{DS} \parallel \overline{AI}$ which gives us $\measuredangle D \cong \measuredangle IAV$ (corresponding angles). Also, since $\overline{IA} \cong \overline{IV}$, $\triangle AIV$ is isosceles, so $\measuredangle IAV \cong \measuredangle V$. The two angle congruence statements allow us to conclude that $\measuredangle D \cong \measuredangle V$.

8.   Yes. By the Triangle Midsegment Theorem (see page 371 in the textbook), since A, W, and K are midpoints of $\overline{TS}$, $\overline{SE}$, and $\overline{ET}$ respectively, $\overline{AW} \parallel \overline{TE}$ and $\overline{KW} \parallel \overline{TS}$. Therefore $TAWK$ is a parallelogram.

Now that the students are familiar with many of the properties of various triangles, quadrilaterals, and special quadrilaterals, they can apply their algebra skills and knowledge of the coordinate grid to study **coordinate geometry**. In this section, the shapes are plotted on a graph. Using familiar ideas, such as the Pythagorean Theorem and slope, the students can prove whether or not quadrilaterals have special properties.

See the Math Notes boxes on pages 378 and 381.

Example 1

On a set of axes, plot the points $A(-3, -1)$, $B(1, -4)$, $C(5, -1)$, and $D(1, 2)$ and connect them in the order given. Is this shape a rhombus? Justify your answer.

To show that this shape is a rhombus, we must show that all four sides are the same length because that is the definition of a rhombus. When we want to find the length of a segment on the coordinate grid, we use the Pythagorean Theorem. To begin, we plot the points on a graph.

Although the shape appears to be a parallelogram, and possibly a rhombus, we cannot base our decision on appearances. To use the Pythagorean Theorem, we outline a **slope triangle** to create a right triangle, using $\overline{AB}$ as the hypotenuse. The lengths of the legs of this right triangle are three and four units. Using the Pythagorean Theorem,

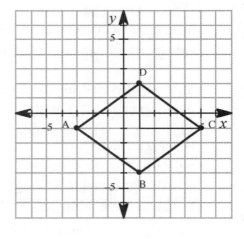

$$3^2 + 4^2 = (AB)^2$$
$$9 + 16 = (AB)^2$$
$$25 = (AB)^2$$
$$AB = 5$$

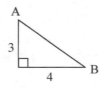

Similarly, we set up slope triangles for the other three sides and use the Pythagorean Theorem again. In each case, we find the lengths are all 5 units. Therefore, since all four sides have the same length, the figure is a rhombus.

Example 2

On a set of axes, plot the points $A(-4, 1)$, $B(1, 3)$, $C(8, -1)$, and $D(4, -3)$, and connect them in the order given. Is this shape a parallelogram? Prove your answer.

When we plot the points, the shape appears to be a parallelogram, or at least close. We cannot base our decision on appearances, however. To prove it is a parallelogram, we must show that the opposite sides are parallel. On the coordinate grid, we show lines are parallel by showing they have the same slope. Once again, we can use slope triangles to find the slope of each side.

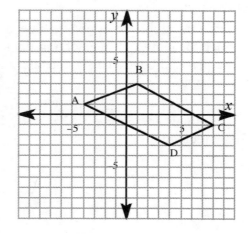

Slope of $\overline{CB} = \frac{4}{-7} = -\frac{4}{7}$

Slope of $\overline{BA} = \frac{2}{5}$

Slope of $\overline{AD} = \frac{-4}{8} = -\frac{1}{2}$

Slope of $\overline{DC} = \frac{2}{4} = \frac{1}{2}$

Although the values are close, the slopes of the opposite sides are not equal. Therefore this is not a parallelogram.

Problems

1.   If $ABCD$ is a rectangle, and $A(1, 2)$, $B(5, 2)$, and $C(5, 5)$, what is the coordinate of D?

2.   If $P(2, 1)$ and $Q(6, 1)$ are the endpoints of the base of an isosceles right triangle, what is the x coordinate of the third vertex?

3.   The three points $S(-1, -1)$, $A(1, 4)$, and $M(2, -1)$ are vertices of a parallelogram. What are the coordinates for three possible points for the other vertex?

4.   Graph the following lines on the same set of axes.

$$y = \frac{3}{5}x + 7 \qquad\qquad y = 0.6x$$
$$y = -\frac{10}{6}x - 1 \qquad\qquad y = -\frac{5}{3}x + 9$$

These lines enclose a shape. What is the name of that shape? Justify your answer.

5.   If $W(-4, -5)$, $X(1, 0)$, $Y(-1, 2)$, and $Z(-6, -3)$, what shape is $WXYZ$? Prove your answer.

6.   If $D(2, 2)$ and $T(6, 4)$, what is the equation of the perpendicular bisector of $\overline{DT}$?

Answers

1.   (1, 5)

2.   4

3.   (4, 4), (0, -6), or (-2, 4)

4.   Since the slopes of opposites side are equal, this is a parallelogram. Additionally, since the slopes of intersecting lines are negative reciprocals of each other, they are perpendicular. This means the angles are all right angles, so the figure is a rectangle.

5.   The slopes are: $\overline{WX}$ = 1, $\overline{XY}$ = -1, $\overline{YZ}$ = 1, and $\overline{ZW}$ = -1. This shows that $WXYZ$ is a rectangle.

6. $y = -2x + 11$

After studying triangles and quadrilaterals, the students now extend their knowledge to all polygons. A polygon is a closed, two-dimensional figure made of three or more non-intersecting straight line segments connected end-to-end. Just as the students were able to determine that the sum of the measures of the angles of a triangle is 180°, the students learn a method to determine the sum of the measures of the interior angles of any polygon. Next they explore the sum of the exterior angles of a polygon. Finally they use the information about the angles of polygons along with their Triangle Toolkit to find the areas of regular polygons.

See the Math Notes boxes on pages 393, 395, 396, 400, 407, 410, and 422.

Example 1

The figure at right is a hexagon. What is the sum of the measures of the interior angles of a hexagon? Explain how you know. Then write an equation and solve for x.

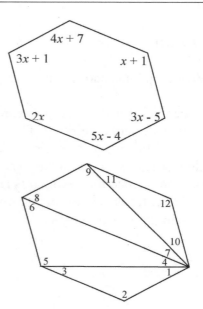

One way to find the sum of the interior angles of the hexagon is to divide the figure into triangles. There are several different ways to do this, but keep in mind that we are trying to add the interior angles at the vertices, so those are the angles we want to see. One easy way to divide the hexagon is to draw in all the diagonals from one vertex as shown at right. Doing this forms four triangles, each with angle measures summing to 180°.

$$\underbrace{m\angle1 + m\angle2 + m\angle3}_{180°} + \underbrace{m\angle4 + m\angle5 + m\angle6}_{180°} + \underbrace{m\angle7 + m\angle8 + m\angle9}_{180°} + \underbrace{m\angle10 + m\angle11 + m\angle12}_{180°}$$
$$= 4(180°) = 720°$$

(Note: students may have noticed that the number of triangles is always two less than the number of sides. This example illustrates why the sum of the interior angles of a polygon may be calculated using $(n-2)180°$, where n is the number of sides of the polygon.) Now that we know what the sum of the angles is, we can write an equation, and solve for x.

$$(3x+1) + (4x+7) + (x+1) + (3x-5) + (5x-4) + (2x) = 720°$$
$$18x = 720°$$
$$x = 40°$$

Example 2

If the sum of the measures of the angles of a polygon is 2340°, how many sides does the polygon have?

Use the equation "sum of interior angles $= (n - 2)180°$" to write an equation and solve for n. The last line gives us an equation that we can solve. Therefore, the polygon has 15 sides. It is important to note that if the an answer is not a whole number, something went wrong. Either we made a mistake or there is no polygon with its interior angles summing to the amount given. Since the answer is the number of sides, the answer can only be a whole number. Polygons cannot have "7.2" sides!

$$(n - 2) \cdot 180° = 2340°$$
$$180n - 360 = 2340$$
$$180n = 2700$$
$$n = 15$$

Example 3

What is the measure of an exterior angle of a regular decagon?

A decagon is a 10-sided polygon. Since this figure is a regular decagon, all the angles and all the sides are congruent. The sum of the measures of the exterior angles of any polygon, one at each vertex, is always 360°, no matter how many sides the polygon has. The exterior angles are congruent since the decagon is regular. The decagon at right has ten exterior angles drawn, one at each vertex. Therefore, each angle measures $\frac{360°}{10} = 36°$.

Example 4

A regular dodecagon (12 sided polygon) has a side length of 8 units. What is its area?

Solving this problem is going to require the use of several topics we have studied. (Note: there is more than one way to solve this problem.) For this solution, we will imagine dividing the dodecagon into 12 triangles, radiating from the center. These triangles are all congruent to each other. If we could find the area of one of them, then we could multiply it by 12 to get the area of the entire figure.

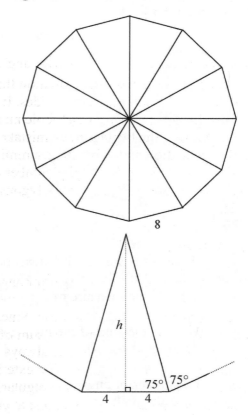

To focus on one triangle, copy and enlarge it. The triangle is isosceles, so drawing a segment from the vertex angle perpendicular to the base gives a height. This height also bisects the base (because this triangle is isosceles).

Since this is a dodecagon, we can find the sum of all the angles of the shape by using the formula the students developed:

$$(12 - 2)(180°) = 1800°$$

Since all the angles are congruent, each angle measures $1800° \div 12 = 150°$. The segments radiating from the center bisect each angle, so the base angle of the isosceles triangle is 75°. Now we can use trigonometry to find h.

$$\tan 75° = \frac{h}{4}$$
$$h = 4 \tan 75°$$
$$h \approx 14.928$$

Therefore the area of one of these triangles is

To find the area of the dodecagon, we multiply the area of one triangle by 12.

$$A \approx \tfrac{1}{2}(8)(14.928)$$
$$A \approx 59.712 \text{ square units}$$

$$A \approx 12(59.712) \approx 716.544 \text{ square units}$$

Problems

1. Using the pentagon at right, write an equation and solve for x.

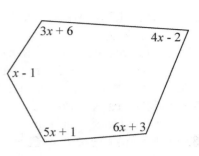

2. Using the heptagon (7-gon) at right, write an equation and solve for x.

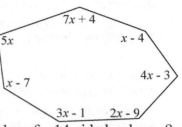

3. What is the sum of the measures of the interior angles of a 14-sided polygon?

4. What is the measure of each interior angle of a regular 16-sided polygon?

5. What is the sum of the measures of the exterior angles, one at each vertex, of a decagon (10-gon)?

6. Each exterior angle of a regular polygon measures 22.5°. How many sides does the polygon have?

7. Does a polygon exist whose sum of the interior angles is 3060°? If so, how many sides does it have? If not, explain why not.

8. Does a polygon exist whose sum of the interior angles is 1350°? If so, how many sides does it have? If not, explain why not.

9. Does a polygon exist whose sum of the interior angles is 4410°? If so, how many sides does it have? If not, explain why not.

10. In the figure at right, $ABCDE$ is a regular pentagon. Is $\overline{EB} \parallel \overline{DF}$? Justify your answer.

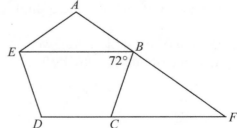

11. What is the area of a regular pentagon with a side length of 10 units?

12. What is the area of a regular 15-gon with a side length of 5 units?

Answers

1. $19x + 7 = 540$,   2. $23x - 20 = 900$,   3. $2160°$
   $x \approx 28.05$ $x = 40$

4. $157.5°$ 5. $360°$ 6.   16 sides

7. 19 sides

8. No. The result is not a whole number. The number of sides must be a whole number.

9. No. The result is not a whole number.

10. Yes. Since *ABCDE* is a regular pentagon, the measure of each interior angle is $108°$. Therefore, $m\angle DCB = 108°$. Since $\angle DCB$ and $\angle FCB$ are supplementary, $m\angle FCB = 72°$. The lines are parallel because the alternate interior angles are congruent.

11. ≈ 172.0 sq. units   12. ≈ 441.1 sq. units

The students return to similarity once again to explore what happens to the area of a figure if it is reduced or enlarged. In Chapter 3, students discussed the ratio of similarity, also called the "zoom factor." If two similar figures have a ratio of similarity of $\frac{a}{b}$, then the ratio of their perimeters is also $\frac{a}{b}$, while the ratio of their areas is $\frac{a^2}{b^2}$.

See the Math Notes boxes on pages 415 and 457.

Example 1

The figures P and Q at right are similar.

a)　　What is the ratio of similarity?

b)　　What is the perimeter of figure P?

c)　　Use your previous two answers to find the perimeter of figure Q.

d)　　If the area of figure P is 34 square units, what is the area of figure Q?

The ratio of similarity is the ratio of the lengths of two corresponding sides. In this case, since we only have the length of one side of figure Q, we will use the side of P that corresponds to that side. Therefore, the ratio of similarity is $\frac{3}{7}$.

To find the perimeter of figure P, add up all the side lengths: $3 + 6 + 4 + 5 + 3 = 21$. If the ratio of similarity of the two figures is $\frac{3}{7}$ then ratio of their perimeters is $\frac{3}{7}$ as well.

$$\frac{\text{perimeter } P}{\text{perimeter } Q} = \frac{3}{7}$$
$$\frac{21}{Q} = \frac{3}{7}$$
$$3Q = 147$$
$$\text{perimeter } Q = 49$$

If the ratio of similarity is $\frac{3}{7}$ then the ratio of the areas is $\left(\frac{3}{7}\right)^2 = \frac{9}{49}$.

$$\frac{\text{area } P}{\text{area } Q} = \left(\frac{3}{7}\right)^2$$
$$\frac{34}{Q} = \frac{9}{49}$$
$$9Q = 1666$$
$$\text{area } Q \approx 185.11 \text{ square units}$$

Example 2

Two rectangles are similar. If the area of the first rectangle is 49 square units, and the area of the second rectangle is 256 square units, what is the ratio of similarity, $\frac{a}{b}$, between these two rectangles?

Since the rectangles are similar, if the ratio of similarity is $\frac{a}{b}$, then the ratio of their areas is $\frac{a^2}{b^2}$. We are given the areas so we know the ratio of their areas is $\frac{49}{256}$. Therefore we can write:

$$\frac{a^2}{b^2} = \frac{49}{256}$$

$$\frac{a}{b} = \sqrt{\frac{49}{256}} = \frac{\sqrt{49}}{\sqrt{256}} = \frac{7}{16}$$

The ratio of similarity between the two rectangles is $\frac{a}{b} = \frac{7}{16}$. This can be written as a decimal or left as is.

Problems

1.   If figure A and figure B are similar with a ratio of similarity of $\frac{5}{4}$, and the perimeter of figure A is 18 units, what is the perimeter of figure B?

2.   If figure A and figure B are similar with a ratio of similarity of $\frac{1}{8}$, and the area of figure A is 13 square units, what is the area of figure B?

3.   If figure A and figure B are similar with a ratio of similarity of 6, that is, 6 to 1, and the perimeter of figure A is 54 units, what is the perimeter of figure B?

4.   If figure A and figure B are similar and the ratio of their perimeters is $\frac{17}{6}$, what is their ratio of similarity?

5.   If figure A and figure B are similar and the ratio of their areas is $\frac{32}{9}$, what is their ratio of similarity?

6.   If figure A and figure B are similar and the ratio of their perimeters is $\frac{23}{11}$, does that mean the perimeter of figure A is 23 units and the perimeter of figure B is 11 units? Explain.

Answers

1. 14.4 un.   2.   832 sq. un.   3.   9 un.   4. $\frac{17}{6}$ 5. $\frac{\sqrt{32}}{\sqrt{9}} \approx \frac{5.66}{3} \approx 1.89$

6. No, it just tells us the ratio. Figure A could have a perimeter of 46 units while figure B has a perimeter of 22 units.

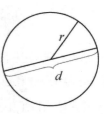

The students have found the area and perimeter of several polygons, triangles, quadrilaterals, pentagons, hexagons, etc. Next they consider what happens to the area as more and more sides are added to a polygon. By exploring the area of a polygon with many sides, they learn that the limit of a polygon is a circle. They extend what they know about the perimeter and area of polygons to circles, and find the relationships for the circumference (C) and area (A) of circles.

$$C = \pi d \text{ or } 2\pi r, \quad A = \pi r^2$$

"C" is the circumference of the circle (a circle's perimeter), "d" is the diameter, and "r" is the radius. "π," which is in both formulas, is by definition the ratio $\frac{circumference}{diameter}$, and it is always a constant for any size circle.

Using these formulas, along with ratios, the students are able to find the perimeter and area of shapes containing parts of circles.

See the Math Notes boxes on pages 426 and 430.

Example 1

The circle at right has a radius of 8 cm. What are the circumference and the area of the circle? Using the formulas,

$$C = 2\pi r \qquad\qquad A = \pi r^2$$
$$= 2\pi(8) \qquad\qquad = \pi(8)^2$$
$$= 16\pi \qquad\qquad = 64\pi$$
$$\approx 50.27 \text{ cm} \qquad\qquad \approx 201.06 \text{ sq. cm}$$

Example 2

Hermione has a small space on her corner lot that she would like to turn into a patio. To do this, she needs to do two things. First, she must know the length of the curved part, where she will put some decorative edging. Second, with the edging in place, she will need to purchase concrete to cover the patio. The concrete is sold in bags. Each bag will fill 2.5 square feet to the required depth of four inches. How much edging and concrete should Hermione buy?

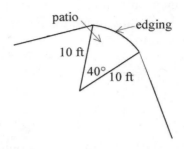

The edging is a portion of the circumference of a circle with the center at point O and a radius of 10 feet. We can determine the exact fraction of the circle by looking at the measure of the central angle. Since the angle measures 40°, and there are 360° in the whole circle, this portion is $\frac{40°}{360°} = \frac{1}{9}$ of the circle. If we find the circumference and area of the whole circle, then we can take $\frac{1}{9}$ of each of those measurements to find the portion needed.

$$C = \tfrac{1}{9}(2\pi r)$$
$$= \tfrac{1}{9}(2 \cdot \pi \cdot 10)$$
$$= \tfrac{20\pi}{9} \approx 6.98 \text{ feet}$$

$$A = \tfrac{1}{9}\pi r^2$$
$$= \tfrac{1}{9} \cdot \pi \cdot (10)^2$$
$$= \tfrac{100\pi}{9} \approx 34.91 \text{ square feet}$$

Hermione should buy 7 feet of edging (most likely it is sold by the foot), and she should buy 14 bags of concrete ($34.91 \div 2.5 \approx 13.96$ bags). Concrete is sold in full bags only.

Example 3

Rubeus' dog Fluffy is tethered to the side of his house at point X. If Fluffy's rope is 18 feet long, how much area does Fluffy have to run in?

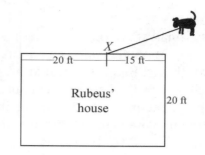

Because Fluffy is tethered to a point by a rope, he can only go where the rope can reach. Assuming that there are no obstacles, this area would be circular. Since Fluffy is blocked by the house, the area will only be a portion of a circle.

From point X, Fluffy can reach 18 feet to the left and right of point X. This initial piece is a semicircle. But, to the right of point X, the rope will bend around the corner of the house, adding a little more area for Fluffy. This smaller piece is a quarter of a circle with a radius of 3 feet.

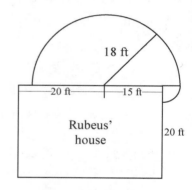

Semicircle:

$A = \frac{1}{2}\pi r^2$

$= \frac{18^2 \pi}{2}$

$= \frac{324\pi}{2}$

$= 162\pi \approx 508.94$

Quarter circle:

$A = \frac{1}{4}\pi r^2$

$= \frac{3^2 \pi}{4}$

$= \frac{9\pi}{4}$

≈ 7.07

Fluffy has a total of $508.94 + 7.07 \approx 516$ square feet in which to run.

Problems

Find the area of the shaded sector in each circle below. In each case, point O is the center.

1.

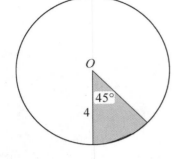

2.

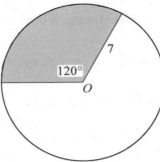

3.

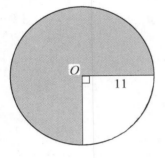

4.

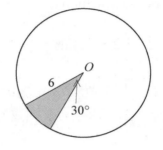

5. Find the perimeter of the shaded sector in problem 1.

6. Find the perimeter of the shaded sector in problem 2.

7. Find the perimeter of the shaded sector in problem 3.

8. Find the perimeter of the shaded sector in problem 4.

9. Kennedy and Tess are constructing a racetrack for their horses. The track encloses a field that is rectangular, with two semicircles at each end. A fence must surround this field. How much fencing will Kennedy and Tess need?

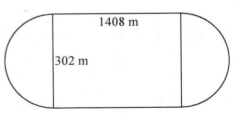

10. Rubeus has moved his dog Fluffy to a corner of his barn because he wants him to have more room to run. If Fluffy is tethered at point X on the barn with a 20 foot rope, how much area does Fluffy have to explore?

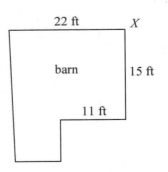

Answers

1. $2\pi \approx 6.28$ square units

2. $\frac{49}{3}\pi \approx 51.31$ square units

3. $\frac{363\pi}{4} \approx 285.10$ square units

4. $3\pi \approx 9.42$ square units

5. $\pi + 8 \approx 11.14$ units

6. $\frac{14\pi}{3} + 14 \approx 28.66$ units

7. $\frac{33\pi}{2} + 22 \approx 73.84$ units

8. $\pi + 12 \approx 15.14$ units

9. $2816 + 302\pi \approx 3764.76$ meters of fencing

10. $200\pi + 100\pi + \frac{25\pi}{4} \approx 962.11$ square feet

In this chapter, the students examine three-dimensional shapes, known as solids. The students will work on visualizing these solids by building and then drawing them. Visualization is a useful, often overlooked skill in mathematics. By drawing solids students gain a better understanding of volume and surface area.

See the Math Notes boxes on pages 448, 452, and 457.

Example 1

The solid at right is built from individual cubes stacked upon each other on a flat surface. (This means that no cubes are "floating.") Create a mat plan representing this solid. What is the volume of this solid?

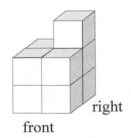

This solid consists of stacked blocks. We are looking at the front, right side, and top of this solid. A mat plan shows a different perspective of a solid. It shows the footprint of the solid as well as how many blocks are in each stack. A mat plan is useful because, in the solid above, we do not know if there are any hidden blocks. A mat plan tells us exactly how many blocks are in the solid.

In this case, since we are creating the mat plan from the stacked blocks, there is more than one possible answer. If there are no hidden blocks, then the mat plan is the first diagram at right. If there is a hidden block, then the mat plan is the second one at right. It is helpful to visualize solids by building them with cubes. Build solids on a 3×5 card so that you can rotate the card to see the solid from all of its sides. Do this to make sure that one block is all that can be hidden in this drawing.

2	3
2	2

front

	1
2	3
2	2

right

The volume of this solid is the number of cubes it would take to build it. In this case, the volume is either 9 cubic units or 10 cubic units.

Example 2

At right is a mat plan of a solid. Build the solid. What is the volume of this solid? Draw the front, right and top views, as well as the three-dimensional view of this solid.

3	2	
2		2
1	1	1

We find the volume by counting the number of blocks it would take to build this solid. Adding the numbers, the volume is 12 cubic units. To draw the different views of this solid, it is extremely helpful to build it out of cubes on a 3 x 5 card. Label the card with front, right, left, and back so that you can remember which side is which when rotating it. Remember that the standard three-dimensional view shows the top, right, and front views.

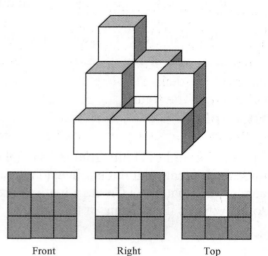

The individual views of each side are flat views. It is helpful to look at the solid at your eye level, so that only one side is visible at a time.

Front   Right   Top

Example 3

If the figure at right is made with the fewest amount of cubes possible, what is its surface area?

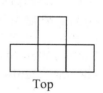

The surface area is the sum of the areas of all the surfaces (or faces or sides) on the solid. If we draw every view of the solid, we can count the number of squares to find the surface area. If we build the solid on a card, then we can rotate the card and count the number of squares on each face. Either way, we will arrive at the same answer.

From the front and back the solid looks the same and shows 10 squares.

The right and left views are reflections of each other and each shows seven squares.

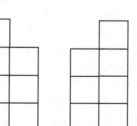

Front/Back   Right   Top

The top and bottom views are also reflections of each other. They show four squares each.

Therefore, the surface area is $10 + 10 + 7 + 7 + 4 + 4 = 42$ square units.

Example 4

The dimensions of the prism at right are shown. What are the volume and surface area of this prism?

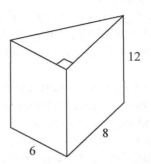

A prism is a special type of polyhedron that has two congruent and parallel bases. In this problem, the bases are right triangles. The volume of a prism is found by finding the area of the base, multiplied by the height of the prism. To understand this process, think of a prism as a stack of cubes. The base area tells you how many cubes are in one layer of the stack. The height tells you how many layers of cubes are in the figure.

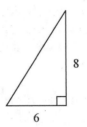

In this example, since the base is a right triangle, the area is $\frac{1}{2}bh$. Looking at the top of the prism might make it easier to find the area of the base represented by A_b.
$A_b = \frac{1}{2}bh = \frac{1}{2}(6)(8) = 24$ square units, so there are 24 cubes in one layer.

To find the volume, we multiply this number by the height, 12.

$$V = A_b h = (24)(12) = 288 \text{ cubic units}$$

To find the surface area of this prism, we will find the area of each of its faces, including the bases, and add the areas. One way to illustrate the subproblems is to make sketches of the surfaces.

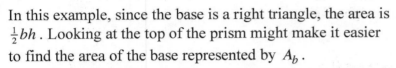

All of the surfaces are familiar shapes, namely, triangles and rectangles. We need to do a subproblem to find the length of the rectangle on the back face (the last rectangle in the pictorial equation above). Fortunately, that length is also the hypotenuse of the right triangle in the base, so we can use the Pythagorean Theorem to find that length.

$$6^2 + 8^2 = c^2$$
$$36 + 64 = c^2$$
$$c^2 = 100$$
$$c = \sqrt{100} = 10$$

Therefore the surface area is:

$$\text{S.A.} = 2\left(\tfrac{1}{2} \cdot 6 \cdot 8\right) + (6 \cdot 12) + (8 \cdot 12) + (10 \cdot 12)$$
$$= 48 + 72 + 96 + 120$$
$$= 336 \text{ square units}$$

Example 5

The Styrofoam pieces used in packing boxes, known as "shipping peanuts," are sold in three box sizes: small, medium and large. The small box has a volume of 1200 cubic inches. The dimensions on the "medium" box are twice the dimensions of the small box, and the "large" box is triple the dimensions of the small one. All three boxes are similar prisms. What are volumes of the medium and large boxes?

Since the boxes are similar, we can use the ratio of similarity to determine the volume of the medium and large boxes without knowing their actual dimensions. When figures are similar with ratio of similarity $\frac{a}{b}$, the ratio of the areas is $\left(\frac{a}{b}\right)^2$ and the ratio of the volumes is $\left(\frac{a}{b}\right)^3$. Since the medium box has dimensions twice the small box and the large box has dimensions three times the small box, we can write:

$$\frac{\text{medium box}}{\text{small box}} = \frac{2}{1}$$

$$\frac{\text{volume of medium box}}{\text{volume of small box}} = \left(\frac{2}{1}\right)^3$$

$$\frac{x}{1200} = \frac{8}{1}$$

$$\frac{\text{large box}}{\text{small box}} = \frac{3}{1}$$

$$\frac{\text{volume of large box}}{\text{volume of small box}} = \left(\frac{3}{1}\right)^3$$

$$\frac{x}{1200} = \frac{27}{1}$$

Solving, $x = 8 \cdot 1200$, $x = 9600$ cubic units   and $x = 27 \cdot 1200$, $x = 32,400$ cubic units.

Problems

For each solid, calculate the volume and surface area, then draw a mat plan. Assume there are no hidden or floating cubes.

1.

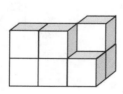

2.

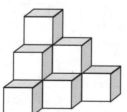

3.

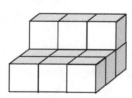

For each mat plan, draw the solid, then calculate the volume and surface area.

4.

	2	2
5	4	1
4	1	1

5.

2	2	1
2		1
1	1	1

6.

3	3	2
	2	2
1	1	1

Calculate the volume and surface area of each prism.

7.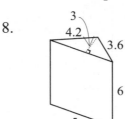

9

5

14

The base is a rectangle.

8.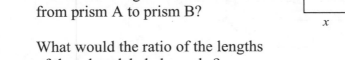

3

4.2

3.6

6

5

9.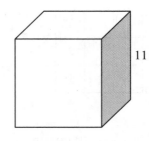

11

A cube.

10. At Cakes R Us, it is possible to buy round cakes in different sizes. The smallest cake has a diameter of 8 inches and a height of 4 inches, and requires 3 cups of batter. Another similar round cake has a diameter of 13 inches. How much batter would this cake require?

11. Prism A and prism B are similar with a ratio of similarity of 2:3. If the volume of prism A is 36 cubic units, what is the volume of prism B?

12. Two rectangular prisms are similar. The smaller, A, has a height of four units while the larger, B, has a height of six units.

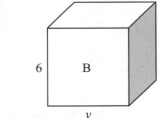

4 A

x

6 B

y

a. What is the magnification factor from prism A to prism B?

b. What would the ratio of the lengths of the edges labeled x and y?

c. What is the ratio of their surface areas? What is the ratio of their volumes?

d. A third prism C is similar to prisms A and B. Prism C's height is ten units. If the volume of prism A is 24 cubic units, what is the volume of prism C?

Answers

1.

		2
2	2	1

V = 7 cu. un.

SA = 28 sq. un.

2.

3	2	1
2	1	
1		

V = 10 cu. un.

SA = 36 sq. un.

3.

2	2	2
1	1	1
1	1	1

V = 12 cu. un.

SA = 38 sq. un.

4. V = 20 cu. un.
SA = 60 sq. un.

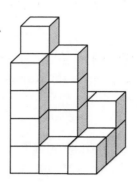

6. V = 15 cu. un.
SA = 46 sq. un.

5. V = 11 cu. un.
SA = 36 sq. un.

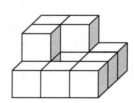

7. V = 630 cu. un.
SA = 482 sq. un.

8. V = 45 cu. un.
SA = 91.8 sq. un.

9. V = 1331 cu. un.
SA = 726 sq. un.

10. ≈ 12.87 cups

11. 121.5 cu. un.

12. a. $\frac{4}{6} = \frac{2}{3}$ b. $\frac{4}{6} = \frac{2}{3}$
c. $\frac{16}{36} = \frac{4}{9}$, $\frac{64}{216} = \frac{8}{27}$
d. 375 cu. un.

Geometry Connections Parent Guide

The remainder of the chapter introduces constructions. Historically, before there were uniform measuring devices, straightedges and compasses were the only means to draw shapes. A straightedge is not a ruler in that it has no measurement markings on it. Despite the fact that the students do not have access to rulers or protractors in this part of the chapter, they are still able to draw shapes, create some specific angle measurements, bisect angles and segments, and copy congruent figures.

See the Math Notes boxes on pages 464, 468, and 471.

Example 1

Using only a straightedge and compass, construct the perpendicular bisector of $\overline{AB}$ at right. Then bisect one of the right angles.

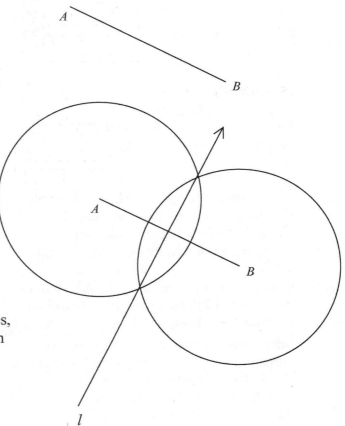

The perpendicular bisector of $\overline{AB}$ is a line that is perpendicular to $\overline{AB}$ and also goes through the midpoint of $\overline{AB}$. Although we could find this line by folding point A onto point B, we want a way to find it with just the straightedge and compass. Also, with no markings on the straightedge, we cannot measure to find the midpoint.

Because of the nature of a compass, circles are the basis for constructions. For this construction, we draw two congruent circles, one with its center at point A, the other with its center at point B. The radii of these circles must be large enough so that the circles intersect at two points. Drawing a line through the two intersection points of intersection gives l, the perpendicular bisector of $\overline{AB}$.

To bisect the right angle, we begin by drawing a circle with a center at point M. There are no restrictions on the length of the radius, but we need to see the points of intersection, P and Q. Also, we are only concerned with the arc of the circle that is within the interior of the angle we are bisecting, $\overset{\frown}{PQ}$. Next we use points P and Q as the centers of two congruent circles that intersect in the interior of $\angle PMQ$. This gives us point X which, when connected to point M, bisects the right angle.

Note: with this construction, we have created two 45° angles. From this we also get a 135° angle, $\angle XMA$. Another bisection (of $\angle XMQ$) would give us a 22.5° angle.

Example 2

Construct $\triangle MUD$ so that $\triangle MUD$ is congruent to $\triangle ABC$ by SAS$\cong$.

To construct a congruent triangle, we will need to use two constructions: copying a segment and copying an angle. In this example we want to construct the triangle with the SAS$\cong$, so we will copy a side, then an angle, and then the adjacent side. It does not matter which side we start with as long as we do the remainder of the parts in a SAS order. Here we will start by copying $\overline{BC}$ with a compass. First draw a ray like the one at right. Next, put the compass point on point B and open the compass so that it reaches to point C. Keeping that measurement, mark off a congruent segment on the ray ($\overline{UD}$). Next copy $\angle BCA$ so that its vertex C is at point D on the ray and one of its sides is $\overline{UD}$. Then copy $\overline{CA}$ to create $\overline{DM}$. Finally, connect point U to point M and $\triangle MUD \cong \triangle ABC$.

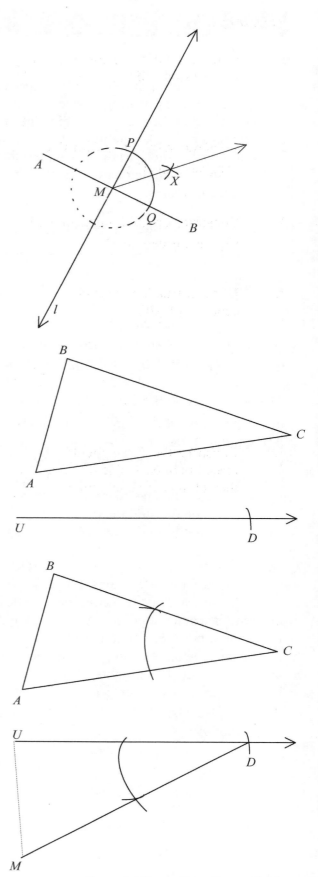

Problems

1. Construct a triangle congruent to $\triangle XYZ$ using SSS$\cong$.

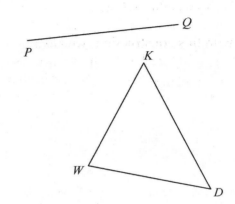

2. Construct a rhombus with sides congruent to $\overline{AB}$.

3. Construct a regular hexagon with sides congruent to $\overline{PQ}$.

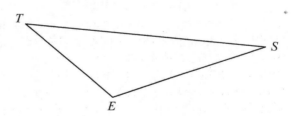

4. Use constructions to find the centroid of $\triangle WKD$.

5. Construct the perpendicular bisectors of each side of $\triangle TES$. Do they all meet in one point?

Answers

1. Draw a ray and copy one side of ΔXYZ on it—for example, $\overline{XZ}$. Copy a second side ($\overline{XY}$), put one endpoint at X, and swing an arc above $\overline{XZ}$. Finally, copy the third side, place the compass point at Z, and swing an arc above $\overline{XZ}$ so that it intersects the arc from X. Connect points X and Z to the point of intersection of the arcs and label it Y.

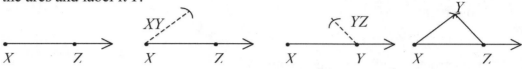

2. Copy $\overline{AB}$ on a ray. Draw another ray from A above the ray and mark a point C on it at the length of $\overline{AB}$. Swing arcs of length AB from B and C and label their intersection D.

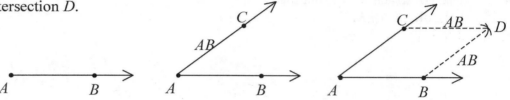

3. Construct a circle of radius $\overline{PQ}$. Mark a point on the circle, then make consecutive arcs around the circle using length PQ. Connect the six points to form the hexagon. Alternately, construct an equilateral triangle using $\overline{PQ}$, then make five copies of the triangle to complete the hexagon.

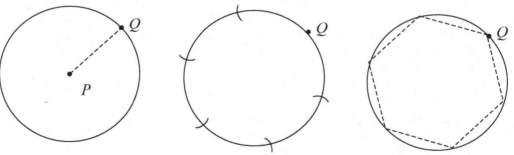

4. Bisect each side of ΔWKD, then draw a segment from each vertex to the midpoint of the opposite side. The point where the medians intersect is the centroid.

5. Yes.

The students revisit circles in the first part of Chapter 10 to develop "circle tools," which will help them find lengths and angle measures within circles. In addition to working with the length of the radius and diameter of a circle, they will add information about angles, arcs, and chords. As with many topics we have studied, this development will utilize triangles.

See the Math Notes boxes on pages 485, 490, 494, 498, and 501.

Example 1

In the circle at right are two chords, $\overline{AB}$ and $\overline{CD}$. Find the center of the circle and label it P.

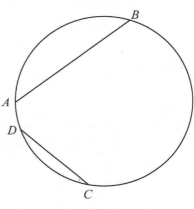

The chords of a circle (segments with endpoints on the circle) are useful segments. In particular, the diameter is a special chord that passes through the center. The perpendicular bisectors of the chords pass through the center of the circle as well. Therefore to find the center, we will find the perpendicular bisectors of each segment. They will meet at the center.

There are several ways to find the perpendicular bisectors of the segments. A quick way is to fold the paper so that the endpoints of the chords come together. The crease will be perpendicular to the chord and bisect it. Another method is to use the construction we learned last chapter. In either case, the point P is the center of the circle.

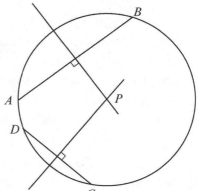

Example 2

In ⊙O at right, use the given information to find the values of x, y, and z.

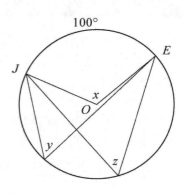

Pieces of a circle are called arcs, and every arc breaks the circle into two pieces. The large piece is called a major arc, and the smaller piece is called a minor arc. Arcs have lengths, and we found lengths of arcs by finding a fraction of the circumference. But arcs also have measures based on the measure of the central angle. In the picture above, ∡JOE is a central angle since its vertex is at the center, O.

An arc's measure is the same as its central angle. Since $\overset{\frown}{JE} = 100°$, $x = 100°$.

An angle with its vertex on the circle is called an inscribed angle. Both of the angles y and z are inscribed angle. Inscribed angles measure half of their intercepted arc (in this case, $\overset{\frown}{JE}$). Therefore, $y = z = \frac{1}{2}(100°) = 50°$.

Example 3

In the figure at right, O is the center of the circle. $\overset{\rightarrow}{TX}$ and $\overset{\rightarrow}{TB}$ are tangent to ⊙O, and $m\angle BOX = 120°$. Find the $m\angle BTX$.

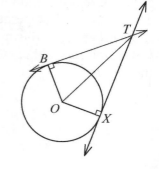

If a line is tangent to a circle, that line intersects the circle in only one point. Also, a radius drawn to the point of tangency is perpendicular to the tangent line. Therefore we know that $\overline{OB} \perp \overline{BT}$ and $\overline{OX} \perp \overline{XT}$. At this point there are different ways to solve this problem. One way is to add a segment to the picture. Adding $\overline{OT}$ will create two triangles, and we know a lot of information about triangles. In fact, these two right triangles are congruent by HL≅ ($\overline{OB} \cong \overline{OX}$ because they are both radii, and $\overline{OT} \cong \overline{OT}$). Since the corresponding parts of congruent triangles are also congruent, and $m\angle BOX = 120°$, we know that $m\angle BOT = m\angle XOT = 60°$. Using the sum of the angles of a triangle is 180°, we find $m\angle BTO = m\angle XTO = 30°$. Therefore, $m\angle BTX = 60°$.

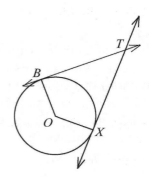

An alternate solution is to note that the two right angles at points B and X, added to ∡BOX, make 300°. Since we know that the angles in a quadrilateral sum to 360°, $m\angle BTX = 360° - 300° = 60°$.

Example 4

In the circle at right, $DV = 9$ units, $SV = 12$ units, and $AV = 4$ units. Find the length of IV.

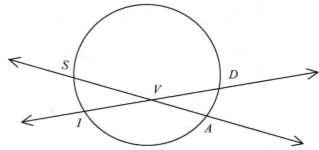

Although we have been concentrating on angles and their measures, there are some facts about lengths of chords of circles that are useful (and should be part of your "circle tools"). In the figure above, if we drew $\overline{SI}$ and $\overline{DA}$ we would form two similar triangles. (See the Math Notes box on page 498.) The sides of similar triangles are proportional, so we can write the proportion at right, which leads to the simplified equation with the two products.

Substitute the lengths that we know, then solve the equation.

$$\frac{SV}{DV} = \frac{IV}{AV}$$
$$SV \cdot AV = DV \cdot IV$$

$$\frac{SV}{DV} = \frac{IV}{AV}$$
$$\frac{12}{9} = \frac{IV}{4}$$
$$9IV = 48$$
$$IV \approx 5.33 \text{ units}$$

Problems

In $\odot O$, $m\widehat{WT} = 86°$ and $m\widehat{EA} = 62°$.

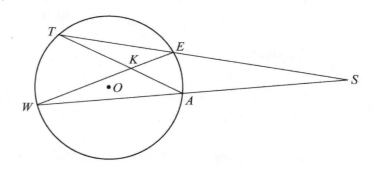

1.   Find $m\angle EWA$.

2.   Find $m\angle WET$.

3.   Find $m\angle WES$.

4.   Find $m\angle WST$.

In $\odot O$, $m\angle EWA = 36°$ and $m\angle WST = 42°$.

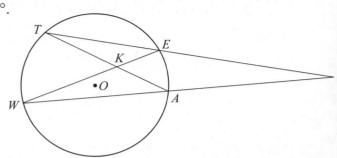

5. Find $m\angle WES$.

6. Find $m\overset{\frown}{TW}$.

7. Find $m\overset{\frown}{EA}$.

8. Find $m\angle TKE$.

9. In the figure at right, $m\overset{\frown}{SD} = 92°$, $m\overset{\frown}{DA} = 103°$, $m\overset{\frown}{AI} = 41°$ and $\overrightarrow{SW}$ is tangent to $\odot O$. Find $m\angle AKD$ and $m\angle VAS$.

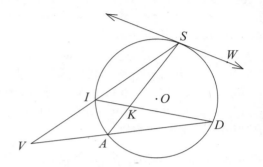

10. In the figure at right, $m\overset{\frown}{EK} = 43°$, $\overline{EW} \cong \overline{KW}$, and $\overrightarrow{ST}$ is tangent to $\odot O$. Find $m\angle WEO$ and $m\angle SEW$.

Answers

1. $\frac{1}{2}(62°) = 31°$

2. $\frac{1}{2}(86°) = 43°$

3. $180° - 43° = 137°$

4. $180° - 137° - 31° = 12°$

5. $180° - 36° - 42° = 102°$

6. $m\angle TEW = 180° - 102° = 78°$, $2(78°) = 156°$

7. $2(36°) = 72°$

8. $180° - 36° - 78° = 66°$

9. $m\angle SAD = \frac{1}{2}(92°)$, $m\angle IDA = \frac{1}{2}(41°)$, $180° - 46° - 20.5° = 113.5°$, $m\angle VAS = 180° - 46° = 134°$

10. $m\angle EWK = \frac{1}{2}(43°) = 21.5°$, $m\angle EOK = 43°$, so $317°$ remain for the other angle at O. $m\angle WEO = m\angle WKO$ and for $WEOK$, $360° - 21.5° - 317° = 21.5° = m\angle WEO + m\angle WKO$, so $m\angle WEO = \frac{1}{2}(21.5°) = 10.75°$. $m\angle SEO = 90°$, $m\angle WEO = 10.75°$, so $m\angle SEW = 79.25°$.

The students next investigate probability and expected value. Utilizing what the students already know about probability, their knowledge is extended, first through collecting data, and then by developing the mathematics behind the problem. Ultimately, the students come up with a formula for calculating the expected value for each play of a game. Something to be careful of in this section: students sometimes think that the expected value must actually be one of the possible outcomes. It does not have to be. The expected value tells what is the average expected result for <u>one</u> play.

See the Math Notes boxes on pages 505 and 516.

Example 1

The spinner at right is divided into different sections, each assigned a different point value. The three smaller sections are congruent. If you were to spin the spinner 100 times, how many times would you expect to get each of the different point values? What is the expected value of this spinner?

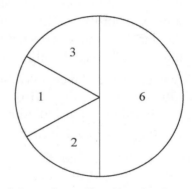

The size of each region is what determines the probability of the spinner landing in that region. Therefore the probability of landing on 6 points is $\frac{1}{2}$ because that region takes up half of the spinner. The other half of the circle is divided into three equal parts, each taking up $\frac{1}{6}$ of the whole spinner ($\frac{1}{3}$ of $\frac{1}{2}$). Now that we know the probabilities, we can determine how many times we would expect the values to come up. Since the probability of getting 6 points is $\frac{1}{2}$, we would expect that about half of the 100 spins would land on the 6, so 50 times. Similarly, since the probability of landing on 1 point (or 2 or 3) is $\frac{1}{6}$, would we expect about $\frac{1}{6}$ of the 100 spins to land on each of those, or about 16 or 17 times. If the total number of spins is 100, we can expect on average about 50 of them to be 6 points, $16\frac{2}{3}$ to be 1 point, $16\frac{2}{3}$ to be 2 points, and $16\frac{2}{3}$ to be 3 points. (Note: these are estimates, not exact or guaranteed.) Using these numbers, after 100 spins, the player would have about $50(6) + 16\frac{2}{3}(1) + 16\frac{2}{3}(2) + 16\frac{2}{3}(3) = 400$ points. If the player earns 400 points in 100 spins, then on average the player received 4 points per spin. So for any single spin, the expected value is four points. Note: four is the expected value for this spinner, but it is NOT one of the possible outcomes.

Example 2

A 3 x 3 grid of nine congruent squares, each with a side length of 2 inches, is painted various colors. Six of the small squares are painted red while three are painted blue. For $1.00 a player can throw a dart at the grid. If the player hits a blue square, he is handed $2.00. Is this a fair game? Justify your answer.

The definition of a "fair" game is one in which the expected value is 0 because this means that, on average, the player is not guaranteed to win, and neither is the person running the game. If the expected value is 0, then winning or losing is just a matter of luck, and the game does not favor one side over the other. To determine if this game is fair we need to calculate its expected value.

Although we could go through a procedure similar to what we did in the last problem, there is a formula that is derived from that procedure that we can use. The expected value is found by summing the products of the amount won and its probability. In this problem, each game costs $1.00. If the dart lands on a red square, the player loses $1.00 (the value is -1). The probability of hitting a red square is $\frac{6}{9} = \frac{2}{3}$. However, if the player hits a blue square, the player receives $2.00, which wins only $1.00 (because he paid $1.00 for the dart). Based on the calculations at right, the expected value

$$E = \frac{2}{3}(-1.00) + \frac{1}{3}(1.00)$$
$$= -\frac{2}{3} + \frac{1}{3}$$
$$= -\frac{1}{3}$$

is $-\frac{1}{3}$ This tells us that on average the player can expect to lose $\frac{1}{3}$ of a dollar, or about $0.33, each turn. Therefore, this is not a fair game; it favors the person running the game (often known as "the house").

Problems

The spinners below have different point values assigned to the different regions. What is the expected value for each spinner? (Assume that regions that appear to be congruent, are congruent.)

1.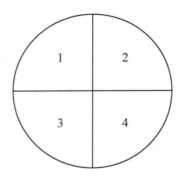

2.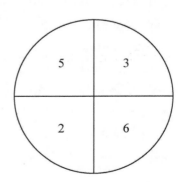

3.

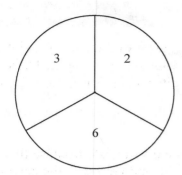

4.

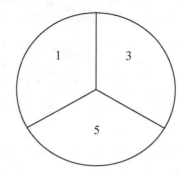

5.

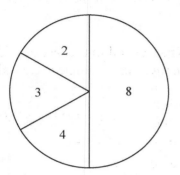

6.

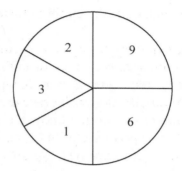

7. For $2.00 a player gets five darts to throw at a board that looks like the figure at right. The board is a square, measuring one foot along each side. The circle is centered and has a diameter of six inches. For each dart that lands in the interior of the circle, the players gets $0.75. Is this game fair? Justify your answer.

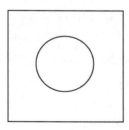

Answers

1. 2.5

2. 4

3. ≈ 3.7

4. 3

5. 5.5

6. 4.75

7. Not fair because the expected value is about −$1.25 .

The students have examined the parts of circles, found measurements of their chords and angles, and have used them with probability and expected value. This section places the circle on the coordinate grid so that the students can derive the equation of a circle.

Example 1

What is the equation of the circle centered at the origin with a radius of 5 units?

The key to deriving the equation of this circle is the Pythagorean Theorem. That means we will need to create a right triangle within the circle. First, draw the circle on graph paper, then choose any point on the circle. We do not know the exact coordinates of this point so call it (x, y). Since endpoints of the radius are $(0,0)$ and (x, y), we can represent the length of the vertical leg as y and the length of the horizontal leg as x. If we call the radius r, then using the Pythagorean Theorem we can write $x^2 + y^2 = r^2$. Since we know the radius is 5, we can write the equation of this circle as $x^2 + y^2 = 5^2$, or $x^2 + y^2 = 25$.

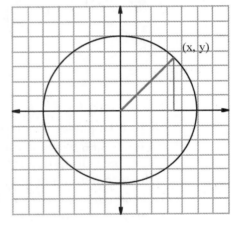

Example 2

Graph the circle $(x-4)^2 + (y+2)^2 = 49$.

Based on what we have seen, this is a circle with a radius of 7. This one, however, is not centered at the origin. The general equation of a circle is $(x-h)^2 + (y-k)^2 = r^2$. The center of the circle is represented by (h, k), so in this example the center is $(4, -2)$ The center of this circle has been shifted four units to the right, and two units down.

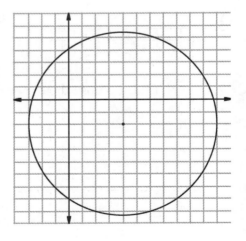

Problems

1. What is the equation of the circle centered at (0, 0) with a radius of 25?

2. What is the equation of the circle centered at the origin with a radius of 7.5?

3. What is the equation of the circle centered at (5, -3) with a radius of 9?

Graph the following circles.

4. $(x+1)^2 + (y+5)^2 = 16$

5. $x^2 + (y-6)^2 = 36$

6. $(x-3)^2 + y^2 = 64$

Answers

1. $x^2 + y^2 = 625$

2. $x^2 + y^2 = 56.25$

3. $(x-5)^2 + (y+3)^2 = 81$

4.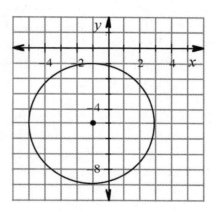

5.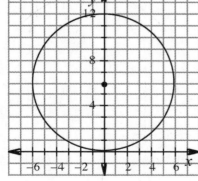

6.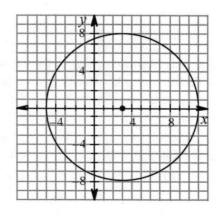

The students have already worked with solids, finding the volume and surface area of prisms and other shapes built with blocks. Now the students extend these skills to find the volume and surface area of pyramids, cones, and spheres.

See the Math Notes boxes on pages 529, 534, 538, 543, and 547.

Example 1

A regular hexahedron has an edge length of 20 cm. What is the surface area and volume of this solid?

Although the name "regular hexahedron" might sound intimidating, it just refers to a regular solid with six (hexa) faces. As defined earlier, regular means all angles are congruent and all side lengths are congruent. A regular hexahedron is just a cube, so all six faces are congruent squares.

To find the volume of the cube, we can use our previous knowledge: find the area of the base and multiply by the height. Since the base is a square, its area is 400 square cm. The height is 20 cm, therefore the volume is 8000 cubic cm.

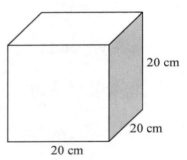

To find the surface area we will find the sum of the areas of all six faces. Since each face is a square and they are all congruent, this will be fairly easy. The area of one square is 400 square cm, and there are six of them. Therefore the surface area is 2400 square cm.

Example 2

The base of the pyramid at right is a regular hexagon. Using the measurements provided, calculate the surface area and volume of the pyramid.

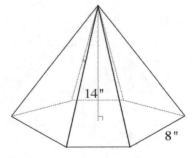

The volume of any pyramid is $V = \frac{1}{3}A_b h$ (h is the height of the pyramid, 14" in this case, and A_b is represents the area of the base). We find the surface area the same way we do for all solids: we find the area of each face and base, then add them all

together. The lateral faces of the pyramid are all congruent
triangles. The base is a regular hexagon. Since we need the area
of the hexagon for both the volume and the surface area, we will
find it first.

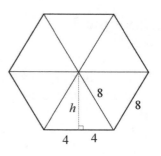

There are several ways to find the area of a regular hexagon.
One way is to cut the hexagon into six congruent equilateral
triangles, each with a side of 8". If we can find the area of one
triangle, then we can multiply by 6 to find the area of the
hexagon. To find the area of one triangle we need to find the
value of h, the height of the triangle. Recall that we studied
these triangles earlier; remember that the height cuts the
equilateral triangle into two congruent 30°-60°-90° triangles. To
find h, we can use the Pythagorean Theorem, or if you
remember the pattern for a 30°-60°-90° triangle, we can use
that. With either method we find that $h = 4\sqrt{3}$". Therefore the
area of one equilateral triangle is shown at right.

$$A = \tfrac{1}{2}bh$$
$$= \tfrac{1}{2} \cdot (8) \cdot \left(4\sqrt{3}\right)$$
$$= 16\sqrt{3} \approx 27.71 \text{ in}^2$$

The area of the hexagon is $6 \cdot 16\sqrt{3} = 96\sqrt{3} \approx 166.28 \text{ in}^2$.
Now find the volume of the pyramid using the formula above.

$$V = \tfrac{1}{3}A_b h$$
$$= \tfrac{1}{3} \cdot \left(96\sqrt{3}\right) \cdot (14)$$
$$= 448\sqrt{3} \approx 776 \text{ in}^3$$

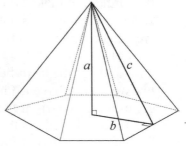

Next we need to find the area of one of the triangular faces.
These triangles are slanted, and the height of one of them is
called a slant height. The problem does not give us the value of
the slant height (labeled c at right), but we can calculate it based
on the information we already have.

A cross section of the pyramid at right shows a right triangle in
its interior. One leg is labeled a, another b, and the hypotenuse
c. The original picture gives us $a = 14$". The length of b we
found previously: it is the height of one of the equilateral
triangles in the hexagonal base. Therefore, $b = 4\sqrt{3}$. To
calculate c, we use the Pythagorean Theorem.

$$a^2 + b^2 = c^2$$
$$14^2 + \left(4\sqrt{3}\right)^2 = c^2$$
$$196 + 48 = c^2$$
$$c^2 = 244$$
$$c = \sqrt{244} = 2\sqrt{61} \approx 15.62"$$

The base of one of the slanted triangles is 8", the length of the
side of the hexagon. Therefore the area of one slanted triangle is
$8\sqrt{61} \approx 62.48 \text{ in.}^2$ as shown at right.

$$A = \tfrac{1}{2} \cdot b \cdot h$$
$$= \tfrac{1}{2} \cdot (8) \cdot \left(2\sqrt{61}\right)$$
$$= 8\sqrt{61} \approx 62.48 \text{ in}^2$$

Since there are six of these triangles, the area of the lateral faces
is $6 \cdot \left(8\sqrt{61}\right) = 48\sqrt{61} \approx 374.89 \text{ in}^2$.

Now we have all we need to find the total surface area: $96\sqrt{3} + 48\sqrt{61} \approx 541.17 \text{ in}^2$.

Example 3

The cone at right has the measurements shown. What is the lateral surface area and volume of the cone?

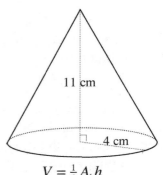

The volume of a cone is the same as the volume of any pyramid: $V = \frac{1}{3}A_b h$. The only difference is that the base is a circle, but since we know how to find the area of a circle ($A = \pi r^2$), we find the volume as shown at right.

$$V = \frac{1}{3}A_b h$$
$$= \frac{1}{3}(\pi r^2)h$$
$$= \frac{1}{3}(\pi \cdot 4^2)\cdot 11$$
$$= \frac{1}{3}\cdot(176\pi) = \frac{176\pi}{3}$$
$$\approx 184.3 \text{ cm}^3$$

Calculating the lateral surface area of a cone is a different matter. If we think of a cone as a child's party hat, we can imagine cutting it apart to make it lay flat. If we did, we would find that the cone is really a sector of a circle – not the circle that makes up the base of the cone, but a circle whose radius is the slant height of the cone. By using ratios we can come up with the formula for the lateral surface area of the cone, $SA = \pi r l$, where r is the radius of the base and l is the slant height. In this problem, we have r, but we do not have l. Find it by taking a cross section of the cone to create a right triangle. The legs of the right triangle are 11 and 4, and l is the hypotenuse. Using the Pythagorean Theorem we have:

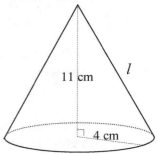

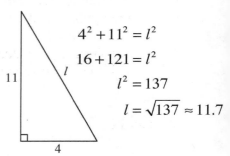

$$4^2 + 11^2 = l^2$$
$$16 + 121 = l^2$$
$$l^2 = 137$$
$$l = \sqrt{137} \approx 11.7$$

Now we can calculate the lateral surface area:
$SA = \pi(4)(11.7) \approx 147.1 \text{ cm}^2$

Example 4

The sphere at right has a radius of 6 feet. Calculate the surface area and the volume of the sphere.

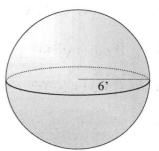

Since spheres are related to circles, we should expect that the formulas for the surface area and volume will have π in them. The surface area of a sphere with radius r is $4\pi r^2$.
Since we know the radius of the sphere is 6,
$$SA = 4\pi(6)^2 = 144\pi \approx 452.39 \text{ ft.}^2$$
To find the volume of the sphere, we use the formula $V = \frac{4}{3}\pi r^3$. Therefore,
$$V = \frac{4}{3}\pi(6)^3 = \frac{4\cdot 216\cdot \pi}{3} = 288\pi \approx 904.78 \text{ ft}^3.$$

Problems

1. The figure at right is a square based pyramid. Calculate its surface area and its volume.

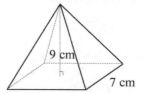

2. Another pyramid, congruent to the one in the previous problem, is glued to the bottom of the first pyramid, so that their bases coincide. What is the name of the new solid? Calculate the surface area and volume of the new solid.

3. A regular pentagon has a side length of 10 in. Calculate the area of the pentagon.

4. The pentagon of the previous problem is the base of a right pyramid with a height of 18. What is the surface area and volume of the pyramid?

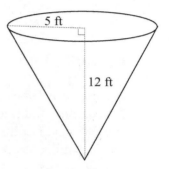

5. What is the total surface area and volume of the cone at right?

6. A cone fits perfectly inside a cylinder as shown. If the volume of the cylinder is 81π cubic units, what is the volume of the cone?

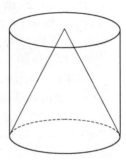

7. A sphere has a radius of 12 cm. What is the surface area and volume of the sphere?

Answers

1. $V = 147$ cm^3, $SA \approx 184.19$ cm^2 2. Octahedron, $V = 294$ cm^3, $SA \approx 270.38$ cm^2

3. $A \approx 172.05$ in^2 4. $V = 1032.29$ in^3, $SA \approx 653.75$ in^2

5. $V \approx 314.16$ ft^3, $SA = 90\pi \approx 282.74$ ft^2

6. 27π cubic units.

7. $SA = 576\pi \approx 1089.56$ cm^2, $V = 2304\pi \approx 7238.23$ cm^3

Throughout the year, the students have varied their study from two-dimensional objects to three-dimensional objects, and back again. This section applies these studies to geometry on a globe. Students learn terms associated with a globe (longitude, latitude, equator, great circle), how the globe is divided, and how to locate cities on it. Additionally, they can find the distance between two cities with the same latitude. Students also notice that some of the facts that are true on flat surfaces change on a curved surface. For instance, it is possible to have a triangle with two right angles on a sphere.

See the Math Notes boxes on pages 551 and 555.

Example 1

If Annapolis, Maryland is at approximately 75° west of prime meridian, and 38° north of the equator, and Sacramento, California is approximately 122° west of prime meridian, and 38° north of the equator, approximate the distance between the two cities. (The Earth's radius is approximately 4000 miles.)

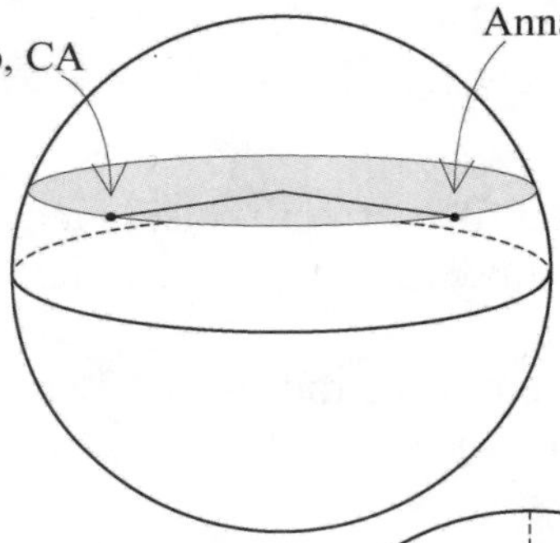

The two cities lie on the same latitude, so they are both on the circumference of the shaded circle. The central angle that connects the two cities is 47° (122° - 75°). This means that the arc length between the two cities is $\frac{47}{360}$ of the circle's circumference. To find the shaded circle's circumference, we must find the radius of the circle.

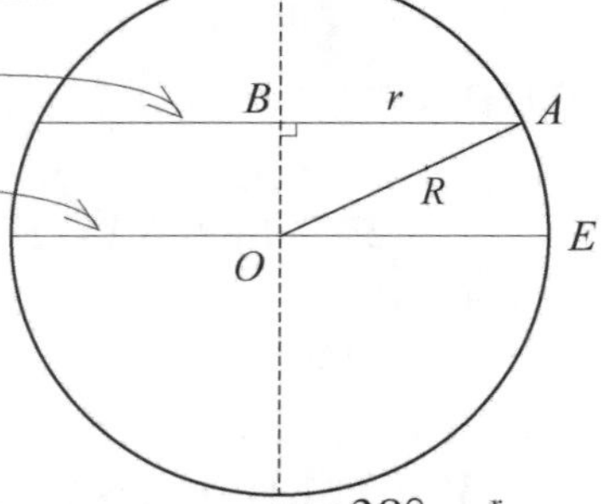

Looking at a cross section of the globe we see something familiar: triangles. In the diagram R is the radius of the Earth while r is the radius of the shaded circle (the one we are trying to find). Since this circle is at 38° north, $m\angle EOA = 38°$. Because the latitude lines are parallel, we also know that $m\angle BAO = 38°$.

$$\cos 38° = \frac{r}{R}$$
$$\cos 38° = \frac{r}{4000}$$
$$r = 4000\cos 38°$$
$$r \approx 3152$$

We use trigonometry to solve for r, as shown at right. This is the radius of the circle on which the two cities lie. Next we find the fraction of its circumference that is the distance, D, between the two cities.

$$D = \frac{47}{360}(2 \cdot \pi \cdot r)$$
$$= \frac{47}{360}(2 \cdot \pi \cdot 3152)$$
$$\approx 2586$$

Therefore the cities are approximately 2586 miles apart.

Problems

1. Lisbon, Portugal is also 38° north of the equator, but it is 9° west of the prime meridian. How far is Annapolis, MD from Lisbon?

2. How far is Sacramento, CA from Lisbon?

3. Port Elizabeth, South Africa is about 32° south of the equator and 25° east of the prime meridian. Perth, Australia is also about 32° south, but 115° east of the prime meridian. How far apart are Port Elizabeth and Perth?

Answers

1. ≈ 3631 miles.

2. ≈ 6216 miles

3. ≈ 5328 miles

There is still more to learn about circles and more information for the students to add to their circle toolkit. In these sections, the students consider lengths of segments and measures of angles formed when tangents and secants intersect within and outside of a circle. Recall that a tangent is a line that intersects the circle in only one point. A secant is a line that intersects the circle in two points. As before, the explanations and justifications for the information they explore are dependent on triangles.

See the Math Notes box on page 560.

Example 1

In the circle at right, $m\widehat{IY} = 60°$ and $m\widehat{NE} = 40°$. What is $m\angle IPY$?

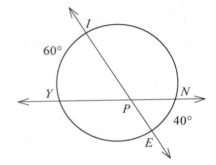

The two lines, $\overleftrightarrow{IE}$ and $\overleftrightarrow{YN}$, are secants since they intersect the circle in two points. When two secants intersect in the interior of the circle, the measure of the angles formed is one-half the sum of the measures of the intercepted arcs, so $m\angle IPY = \frac{1}{2}\left(m\widehat{IY} + m\widehat{NE}\right)$ since $\widehat{IY}$ and $\widehat{NE}$ are the intercepted arcs for this angle. Therefore:

$$m\angle IPY = \frac{1}{2}\left(m\widehat{IY} + m\widehat{NE}\right)$$
$$= \frac{1}{2}\left(60° + 40°\right)$$
$$= 50°$$

Example 2

In the circle at right, $m\widehat{OA} = 140°$ and $m\widehat{RH} = 32°$. What is $m\angle OCA$?

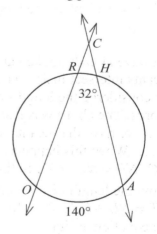

This time the secants intersect outside the circle at point C. When this happens, the measure of the angle is one-half the difference of the measures of the intercepted arcs. Therefore:

$$m\angle OCA = \frac{1}{2}\left(m\widehat{OA} - m\widehat{RH}\right)$$
$$= \frac{1}{2}\left(140° - 32°\right)$$
$$= 54°$$

Example 3

$\overrightarrow{MI}$ and $\overrightarrow{MK}$ are tangent to the circle. $m\overset{\frown}{ILK} = 199°$ and $MI = 13$. Calculate $m\overset{\frown}{IK}$, $m\angle IMK$, and the length of $\overline{MK}$.

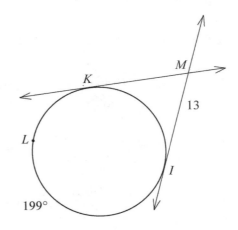

When tangents intersect we have a similar result as we did with the secants. Here, the measure of the angle is again one-half the difference of the measures of the intercepted arcs. But before we can find the measure of the angle, we first need to find $m\overset{\frown}{IK}$. Remember that there are a total of 360° in a circle, and here the circle is broken into just two arcs. If $m\overset{\frown}{ILK} = 199°$, then $m\overset{\frown}{IK} = 360° - 199° = 161°$. Now we can find $m\angle IMK$.

$$m\angle IMK = \tfrac{1}{2}\left(m\overset{\frown}{ILK} - m\overset{\frown}{IK}\right)$$
$$= \tfrac{1}{2}(199° - 161°)$$
$$= 19°$$

Lastly, when two tangents intersect, the segments from the point of intersection to the point of tangency are congruent. Therefore, $MK = 13$.

Example 4

In the figure at right, $DO = 20$, $NO = 6$, and $NU = 8$. Calculate the length of $\overline{UT}$.

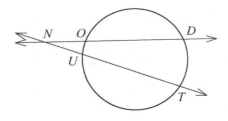

We have already looked at what happens when secants intersect inside the circle. (We did this when we considered the lengths of parts of intersecting chords. The chord was just a portion of the secant.) Now we have the secants intersecting outside the circle. When this happens, we can write $NO \cdot ND = NU \cdot NT$. In this example, we do not know the length of $\overline{UT}$, but we do know that $NT = NU + UT$. Therefore we can write and solve the equation at right.

$$NO \cdot ND = NU \cdot NT$$
$$6 \cdot (6 + 20) = 8 \cdot (8 + UT)$$
$$156 = 64 + 8UT$$
$$92 = 8UT$$
$$UT = 11.5$$

Problems

1. If $m\widehat{ADC} = 212°$, what is $m\angle AEC$?

2. If $m\widehat{AB} = 47°$ and $m\angle AED = 47°$, what is $m\widehat{AD}$?

3. If $m\widehat{ADC} = 3 \cdot m\widehat{AC}$ what is $m\angle AEC$?

4. If $m\widehat{AB} = 60°$, $m\widehat{AD} = 130°$, and $m\widehat{DC} = 110°$, what is $m\angle DEC$?

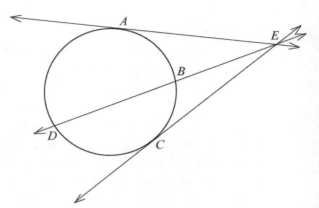

5. If $\overleftrightarrow{RN}$ is a tangent, $RO = 3$, and $RC = 12$, what is the length of $\overline{RN}$?

6. If $\overleftrightarrow{RN}$ is a tangent, $RC = 4x$, $RO = x$, and $RN = 6$, what is the length of $\overline{RC}$?

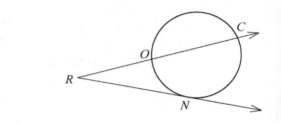

7. If $\overrightarrow{LT}$ is a tangent, $LU = 16$, $LN = 5$, and $LA = 6$, what are the lengths of $\overline{LW}$ and $\overline{NU}$?

8. If $\overrightarrow{TY}$ is a tangent, $BT = 20$, $UT = 4$, and $AT = 6$, what is the length of $\overline{EA}$ and $\overline{BE}$?

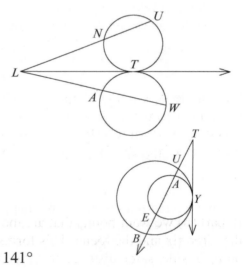

Answers

1. $32°$

2. $141°$

3. $90°$

4. $25°$

5. 6

6. 12

7. $LW = \frac{40}{3}$ and $NU = 11$

8. $EA = \frac{22}{3}$ and $BE = \frac{20}{3}$

This chapter will require skills and knowledge from many earlier chapters. In Chapter 11, the students saw cross sections of different solids when they were finding the radius needed to find the distance between two cities as well as when they found the lengths of slant heights in pyramids. In this chapter we look at different cross sections of cones, which produce several different type of curves. These curves are known as conic sections.

See the Math Notes boxes on pages 578, 585, and 589.

Example 1

Use Focus-Directrix paper for each part, (a) through (c) below, to: (1) highlight the focus at the origin, (2) highlight the directrix 6 units away, and (3) graph the resulting curve. What is the name of each conic section you created?

a.   The points that are twice the distance from the directrix as the focus.

b.   The points that are the same distance from the directrix as they are from the focus.

c.   The points that are six units from the focus.

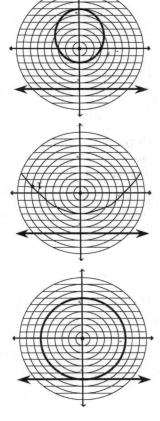

For part (a), if we find all the points that are twice the distance from the directrix as from the focus, we form an ellipse. To check, look at point A. It is six units from the directrix, but only three units from the focus.

In part (b) we want points that are the same distance from both the directrix and the focus. This forms a parabola. Check that point B is the same distance from the focus and the directrix.

In part (c), the points that are just six units from the focus is a circle with a center at the focus and a radius of six.

Example 2

Using what you have learned about the equations of conic sections, state whether the graph of the equation will be a parabola, circle, ellipse or hyperbola.

a. $(x+3)^2 + (y-1)^2 = 100$

b. $y = 3x^2 - 8$

c. $x^2 - 4y^2 = 24$

d. $6x^2 + 3y^2 = 12$

The key to determining which type of graph the equation represents is remembering general forms of equations. Some general forms are:

Parabola: $y = a(x-h)^2 + k$

Ellipse: $a(x-h)^2 + b(y-k)^2 = c$

Circle: $(x-h)^2 + (y-k)^2 = r^2$

Hyperbola: $a(x-h)^2 - b(y-k)^2 = c$

In each of these general forms, the variables are x and y, while a, b, and c are constants. These general equations can be written in slightly different forms, so you might see variations of them in another math textbook. The differences that distinguish these equations are:

Parabola: exactly one variable is squared.

Circle: Both variables are squared and they do not have coefficients (constants in front of the variable).

Ellipse: Both variables are squared and at least one variable has a coefficient not equal to 1, the coefficients of x and y are not equal to each other, and the two variable expressions are summed.

Hyperbola: Same as the ellipse except that one variable expression is subtracted from the other.

With this in mind, we can identify the equations above. The equation in part (a) is a circle. From our previous work, we also know that the center of the circle is (-3, 1), and the radius is 10.

The equation in part (b) is a parabola. Only the x is squared and its coefficient is not zero.

The equation in part (c) is a hyperbola. Both variables are squared and one is subtracted from the other.

Lastly, the equation in part (d) is an ellipse. Both variables are squared, their coefficients are different, and the variable expressions are added.

Problems

1. Draw a double cone solid similar to the one at right. For each of the conic sections, draw the cross section that produces that curve.

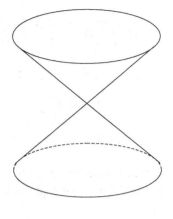

For problems 2 through 4, use a piece of Focus-Directrix paper to highlight a focal point, then highlight a line five units away to be the directrix.

2. Plot three points that are the same distance from the focus as the directrix. What curve do these points lie on?

3. Plot three points that are farther away from the focus than they are from the directrix. What curve do these points lie on?

4. Plot three points that are farther away from the directrix than the focus. What curve do these points lie on?

For each equation below, what is the name of the graph that the equation represents?

5. $y - x^2 = 16$

6. $x^2 + y = 24$

7. $2x^2 + y^2 = 18$

8. $\frac{(x+3)^2}{25} + \frac{(y-7)^2}{25} = 1$

9. $(y-4)^2 - x^2 = 121$

10. $\frac{(x+3)^2}{8} + \frac{(y-7)^2}{6} = 1$

Answers

1. The figure at right shows all cross sections.

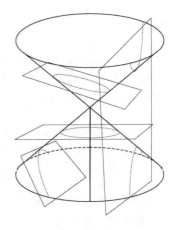

2. A parabola

3. A hyperbola

4. An ellipse

5. A parabola

6. A parabola

7. An ellipse

8. A circle (Multiply both sides of the equation by 25 to make this look more like the general equation of a circle.)

9. A hyperbola

10. An ellipse (No matter what you multiply both sides of the equation by, there will still be a coefficient for the x or y.)

ATLAS OF TUMOR PATHOLOGY

Third Series
Fascicle 3

TUMORS OF THE UTERINE CORPUS AND GESTATIONAL TROPHOBLASTIC DISEASE

by

STEVEN G. SILVERBERG, M.D.
Department of Pathology
George Washington University School of Medicine
Washington, D.C. 20037

and

ROBERT J. KURMAN, M.D.
Department of Pathology
Johns Hopkins Hospital
Baltimore, Maryland 21205

Published by the
ARMED FORCES INSTITUTE OF PATHOLOGY
Washington, D.C.

Under the Auspices of
UNIVERSITIES ASSOCIATED FOR RESEARCH AND EDUCATION IN PATHOLOGY, INC.
Bethesda, Maryland
1992

Accepted for Publication
1991

Available from the American Registry of Pathology
Armed Forces Institute of Pathology
Washington, D.C. 20306-6000
ISSN 0160-6344
ISBN 1-881041-01-8

ATLAS OF TUMOR PATHOLOGY

EDITOR
JUAN ROSAI, M.D.
Department of Pathology
Memorial Sloan-Kettering Cancer Center
New York, New York 10021-6007

ASSOCIATE EDITOR
LESLIE H. SOBIN, M.D.
Armed Forces Institute of Pathology
Washington, D.C. 20306-6000